Soft furnishings

PART TWO

Cushions   Covers   Table Linen

Written and compiled by
Sharyn Skrabanich

A J.B. Fairfax Press Publication

Introduction

❖

*I*t is the special touches, often lovingly made by hand, which give your home its unique quality. Simple discount store furniture can be raised to the level of designer elegance with a sumptuous group of trimmed cushions. Wonderful table linen can disguise an old table that has seen better days. And the good news is – you can do it all yourself.

Stores specialising in furniture fabrics present a dazzling array from which to choose and, for each fabric, there is a further range of possible trimmings.

Take care to plan your design before you begin. Examine the possibilities of colour and texture; assess the needs of your household; explore the fabric stores and collect swatches and samples; and, most importantly, follow your own tastes and preferences.

In **Soft Furnishings, Book One**, you learned all about curtains, blinds and bed linen. In **Soft Furnishings, Book Two**, you will find simple instructions for making and trimming cushions, sewing new covers for furniture, making table linen and, finally, how to add those special finishing touches. Making it yourself can not only transform your home and impress your friends, but gives you enormous satisfaction at the same time.

EDITORIAL
Managing Editor: Judy Poulos
Editorial Assistant: Ella Martin
Editorial Coordinator: Margaret Kelly

PHOTOGRAPHY
Andrew Payne
Additional photography by Andrew Elton

ILLUSTRATIONS
Carol Dunn

DESIGN AND PRODUCTION
Managers: Sheridan Carter, Anna Maguire
Cover design and book design concept:
Michelle Withers
Layout: Margie Mulray, Lulu Dougherty,
Sheridan Packer

Published by J.B. Fairfax Press Pty Limited
80-82 McLachlan Ave
Rushcutters Bay, NSW 2011 Australia
A.C.N 003 738 430

Formatted by J.B. Fairfax Press Pty Limited
Printed by Toppan Printing Co, Singapore

SOFT FURNISHINGS
Part Two: Cushions, Covers, Table Linen
Includes Index
ISBN 1 86343 163 2

DISTRIBUTION AND SALES
Newsagents Direct Distributors
150 Bourke Rd, Alexandria NSW 2015
Ph: (02) 353 9911 Fax: (02) 669 2305

Sales Enquiries:
J.B. Fairfax Press Pty Limited
Ph: (02) 361 6366 Fax: (02) 360 6262

Contents

❖

Creating Your Style

You can achieve the million-dollar effects so admired by the glossy magazines at a tiny fraction of the cost. Before you begin, take the time to do a little research and make some detailed plans.

Colour

Colour is the basis to any room setting. Your colour selections will invoke a certain atmosphere within a room, so it is important to work with colours that reflect the mood you are trying to create. Ruby red, for example, creates a feeling of warmth and passion, whilst subtle, refreshing blue creates a sense of calm and coolness.

The effect of one colour in relation to another can also have a major bearing on your final colour scheme. In some instances, heavily patterned and dyed fabrics absorb surrounding colours into them, totally washing them out.

To decide what kind of effect you want to create, you must consider the features of your room. The positive features should be highlighted and brought to the forefront through the use of suitably coloured or textured fabrics.

Fabrics & fabric selection

Today, home decorators have a vast selection of fabric styles from which to select.

Remember when purchasing fabric, do not skimp on the amount. A full-bodied curtain which flows on to the floor below, makes a grand statement. If you feel the cost of making such a statement could be out of your price range, shop around! Fabric suppliers are usually happy to help you compare prices and quality and you will be surprised at the amount of variation. This is also an opportunity to be creative – lashings of unbleached calico or cotton, used extravagantly, will often create as much ambience as a more expensive fabric.

Golden rules for choosing fabrics

1 Be certain that the fabric you choose is suitable for its intended use. For example, don't expect a shiny chintz to be long-lasting in a child's bedroom or lace covers to resist dirt.

2 Be sure you are making an economically sound purchase. Don't spend loads of money on areas that don't warrant the expense, but do invest in a good quality fabric for high-traffic areas or for pieces of classic design.

3 If you are going to sew soft furnishings, be sure that your machine can sew your chosen fabric.

4 Look into how you plan to care for the fabric and make sure the one you have chosen is suitable for this regime. For example, if you are going to wash your furniture covers at home rather than have them professionally cleaned, be sure that your fabric is washable and will not shrink or distort.

Left: The sample board
Below: The uncluttered simplicity of this living room is enhanced by the choice of fabrics

Trims

Decorative trims provide the finishing touch to many soft furnishing projects.

Most stockists of furnishing fabrics have a good range of trims for you to choose from, and many are surprisingly inexpensive.

For the best results when selecting trims, ensure that the trims and the fabric are similar or compatible in weight, wearability and the type of care they require.

It is sometimes a good idea to purchase right at the beginning, more braid, ribbon or lace than you need, to allow for replacement of worn areas later on.

Pattern

Coordination of patterns is now a breeze for home decorators with many top fabric manufacturers providing totally coordinated ranges to choose from.

Whilst there are no set rules for coordinating fabrics there are some general guidelines for you to refer to. For example, larger scale prints work best when used over larger pieces such as lounge suites or for drapes in larger rooms; vertical stripes will emphasise the height of a wall or window area; smaller florals are ideal for cushions and accents; and plain fabrics in complementary colours make ideal companions for prints.

Making a sample board, such as the ones pictured here, will help you to see how the patterns and colours work together. Keep your samples in the same proportions as they would be in the room.

Top left: The sample board
Right: Combine different prints with a common colour for an interesting visual effect

Pattern matching

When you are using patterned fabric where lengths are joined, you must take care that the patterns match. To do this, you must determine the pattern repeat. A pattern repeat is the length of the pattern, running down the length of a fabric. If your fabric has a strong horizontal motif, it is a good idea to place a complete motif at the top and, if possible, another one at the bottom. If there is a strong motif running vertically through the fabric, the motif should be centred, if possible.

Obviously, you will not always be

Below: The sample board
Bottom: Rich colours are a feature of this stylish bedroom

able to have a complete pattern repeat at the top and at the bottom. The broken repeat should be where it is least visible. Place a medallion or complete pattern repeat in a central position (fig. 1).

Pattern matching & joining panels

To match patterns

1 Cut the first fabric piece from the length of the fabric, placing the beginning of a pattern repeat at the top edge, and lay it flat on a table. Mark the pattern repeat with two pins or tailors chalk and fold under the selvages.

2 Before cutting the second length of fabric, find the beginning of the next pattern repeat and measure your required length from this point, allowing for any necessary seam allowance above this point.

3 Fold in the selvages and baste the two pieces together so that the repeats are matching. Continue, adding as many lengths as you require in this way.

4 Trim the top and bottom edges to be even at the correct length when all the lengths are joined.

Joining panels

Ideally, fabric panels should be joined in such a way that the stitching is as unobtrusive as possible.

1 Place the two panels together with right sides facing. Stitch them together with a 1.5 cm seam and press the seam flat (fig. 2).

2 Trim the seam allowance on one side back to 3 mm and turn in 3 mm on the raw edge of the other seam allowance (figs 3 and 4).

3 Press the folded edge over to the seam line on the other fabric piece, enclosing the raw edges. Slipstitch the folded edge over the previous stitching (fig. 5).

Each print poses a different challenge when it comes to pattern matching

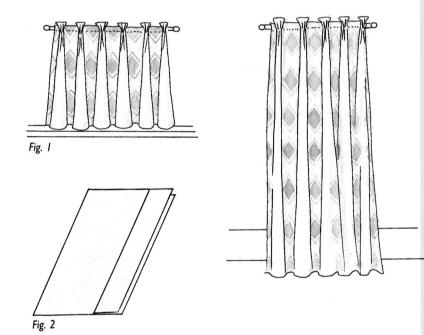

Fig. 1

Fig. 2

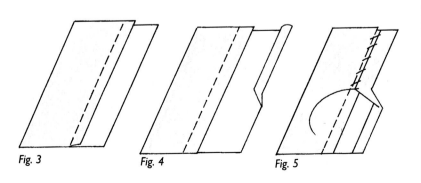

Fig. 3   Fig. 4   Fig. 5

Binding

Making continuous bias binding

1 Cut a piece of bias fabric (fig. 6). Decide on the width of your bias strip, including seam allowances, and mark the bias strips as shown.
2 Fold the fabric with the right sides together, so that both points A and both points B are matching. Note that one strip width extends on each side. Join AA to BB with a 6 mm seam. Press the seam open. Cut along the marked line for the bias strip (fig. 7).

Making and joining strips of bias binding

1 To find the bias on a piece of fabric, fold in one corner so that the top edge is parallel to the selvage. Press the fold. This pressed line is the bias. Draw in lines parallel to the pressed line, the desired width of the bias strip apart. Cut along these lines.
2 Join two strips by placing one length of bias right side up and the second length of fabric wrong side up across each other at an angle of 45 degrees, with the raw edges matching at the end (fig. 8).
3 Stitch the ends together as shown. Press the seam open.

Attaching the binding

Fold the bias strip in half lengthways with the wrong sides facing and place it over both raw edges of the seam. If you are using bias binding you have made yourself, you will need to fold the raw edges under before you pin it in position. Pin and stitch the bias strip into place inside the seam allowance, catching both sides of the bias in the seam (fig. 9).

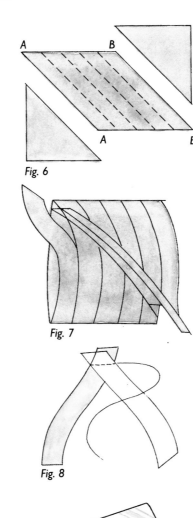

Fig. 6

Fig. 7

Fig. 8

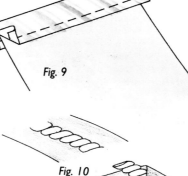

Fig. 9

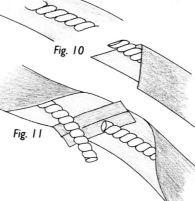

Fig. 10

Fig. 11

Piping

To make piping

1 Make the required length of continuous bias binding. Remember, the bias strip must be wide enough to wrap around the piping cord, leaving sufficient seam allowances on both sides for the stitching.
2 Measure the length of piping you will require for your project. Cords can be joined, if necessary, by butting two ends together and binding them with matching thread or by carefully intertwining the strands (figs 10 and 11).
3 Fold the bias strip over the piping cord. Using matching sewing thread and the zipper foot on your sewing machine, stitch through both sides of the bias strip, stitching close to the cord.

Attaching piping

1 With the right side of one fabric piece facing upwards, lay the piping on top so that the raw edges of the binding match with the raw edge of the fabric and the covered cord lies on the fabric. Baste into position.
2 Place the other piece of fabric right side down, over the top of the other fabric and piping, so that all the raw edges are matching. Stitch along the seam line, securing all the layers of fabric and piping, again using the zipper foot and stitching close to the cord. If necessary, trim the seam allowances to remove any excess bulk.
3 Fold the fabrics right side out with the piping fixed securely between the layers of fabric.

Corners

❖

Corners can be a little tricky to sew neatly, so it's worthwhile taking a moment to learn a trick or two.

Sewing a mitred corner

Mitred corners give a particularly neat square finish to your corners.

1 To sew a mitred corner, press in 3 mm on both raw edges to neaten them, then press in the seam allowances (fig. 1).

2 Open out the corner and press it in towards the centre so that the pressed lines are matching. Press the diagonal; this will be your stitching line (fig. 2).

3 Open out the corner again and refold it diagonally through the corner. Stitch along the diagonal line. Trim the corner, cutting off the excess fabric (fig. 3). Turn the corner right side out and press carefully.

Sewing a mitred corner on a trim

1 Fold the trim over double with the wrong sides together so the raw edges are matching. Pick up the top piece and fold it to one side, so that its edges are now at right angles to the edges of the lower piece and you have formed a diagonal fold. Finger-press the fold (fig. 4)

2 On the wrong side, pin and stitch diagonally from the corner to the edge along the fold, then cut away the excess fabric, so that the corner lies flat. Press the seam open (figs 5 and 6).

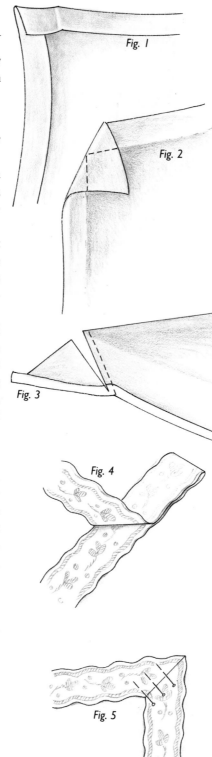

Fig. 1

Fig. 2

Fig. 3

Fig. 4

Fig. 5

Frills & ruffles

❖

Frills and ruffles are one of the easiest decorating finishes for a variety of soft furnishing projects.

Making a ruffle

1 Cut out a strip for the ruffle, adding 3 cm for the bottom hem. If you need to join strips to achieve the full length, add 1.5 cm for each joining seam allowance.

2 Double hem the bottom edge of the ruffle. To gather the ruffle, handsew or machine-sew two parallel rows of gathering stitches across the raw edge in the seam allowance.

Applying an even ruffle

There is a technique to ensure that the ruffling looks even on your finished project.

1 Marking with pins, divide the length of the ruffle into equal parts and then divide the edge to which it will be applied into the same number of equal parts. For smaller projects, four divisions are usual, but for larger projects and circles, six equal parts may be required. If you are attaching the ruffle to a cushion, use the four corners as your marks.

2 Pin the ruffle on, matching the pin marks and adjusting the gathering evenly between them. Pin and baste, then stitch the ruffle into place.

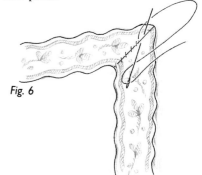

Fig. 6

Seams

Flat seam (figs 7 and 8)

Place the fabrics with right sides together. Stitch the seam with the required seam allowance. Trim the seam if necessary, then press it open.

Flat fell seam (figs 7 to 9)

Place the fabrics with right sides together. Stitch the seam with a 12 mm seam allowance. Trim the seam on one side back to 6 mm, then press the seam open. Fold over the raw edge on the longer side then fold it again, covering the shorter side and enclosing the seam allowances. Stitch down close to the folded edge.

French seam (figs 10 to 13)

Place the fabrics together with the wrong sides facing. Stitch the seam with a 1 cm seam allowance. Trim the seam allowance back to about 5 mm. Fold the fabrics along the seam line so that the right sides are facing. Stitch the seam, 1 cm from the folded edge, enclosing the raw edges of the first seam as you sew. Press the seam to one side.

Zigzag (fig. 14)

This stitch is most commonly used to neaten raw edges on seams. Select the stitch width and length that best suits your fabric.

Edgestitched seams (fig. 15)

Stitch the seam in the ordinary way (see flat seam) and press open the seam allowances. Turn under 3 mm on both raw edges and stitch close to the folded edge keeping the main fabric free.

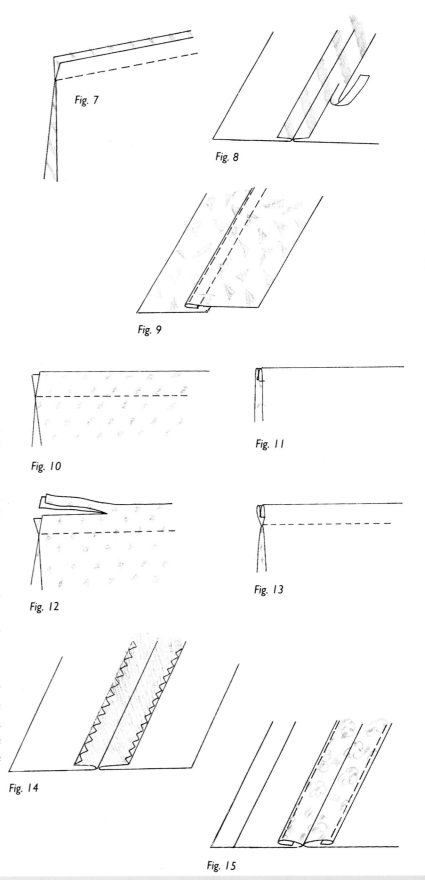

Fig. 7

Fig. 8

Fig. 9

Fig. 10

Fig. 11

Fig. 12

Fig. 13

Fig. 14

Fig. 15

Cushions

Cushions

A SIMPLE CUSHION HAS THE POTENTIAL TO PULL A DECORATIVE SCHEME TOGETHER THROUGH ITS COLOUR, PRINT, STYLE AND EMBELLISHMENTS.

Versatile cushions will transform a tired corner into a focal point of the room, give your chair or sofa a new look, or make a hard chair inviting and comfortable. As well as adding finishing touches, large cushions can provide valuable extra seating.

Choosing the style for your cushions is a matter of personal taste combined with consideration of the intended use of the cushion. This balance will determine whether you are trying to achieve a crisp, neatly defined look with straight piping or single lengths of braid, or a totally feminine look with ruffles and lace frills. Your choice of trims will give your cushion a unique touch. Experiment with some of the ideas in this chapter, mixing and matching ideas for different effects.

Fabrics and fillings

The selection of fabric for cushions will depend upon their end use. Durable fabrics are required for floor cushions and loose covers; lace and delicate broderie anglaise should be used only for purely decorative cushions; whilst general furnishing fabrics are ideal for all types of scatter cushions.

For the dining and kitchen areas use easy-care fabrics that can be thrown into the washing machine time and time again. Fabrics that are in constant use, such as in the family room, can be treated with one of the stain-repellent sprays, such as Scotchgard or Teflon. These products need to be reapplied after each wash. Upholstery-weight fabrics often come already impregnated with a similar product, offering immediate protection.

Fillings should be chosen carefully. Use feather or down fillings only with tightly woven fabrics; fabrics which are loosely woven will allow the feathers or down to migrate through. (Fine cotton or chintz is ideal for casings for down or feather fillings.) Foam chips are less expensive than feathers or down, but are lumpy and will crumble over time. Foam blocks can be cut to any shape or size. Polyester fibre is fully washable, inexpensive and easy to work with, giving a final product that is soft and pliable.

Trimming cushions

❖

Cushions can be embellished in a number of ways.

In this section, you will find many of these methods of trimming described in detail. Use them alone or combined to create cushions with a unique touch.

Continuous corded piping

Piping is one of the most frequently used ways of trimming cushion covers. It can be used alone or combined with ruffles, made from the same fabric as the cushion cover or from a contrasting one.

Begin by making the required length of continuous corded piping in the manner described on page 7.

To attach the piping:

1 With the right sides of the piping and the fabric facing and the raw edges matching, pin the piping around the edge of the cushion cover front, clipping the piping seam allowances at the corners to allow the piping to curve more easily.

2 Cut 2 cm of the piping cord out of one end of the piping to lessen the bulk at the overlap. Overlap the ends of the piping. Stitch as close to the piping cord as possible, using the zipper foot on your sewing machine.

Ready-made trims

To save time and still create a truly beautiful cushion, invest in one of the many bullion trims that are available from retail outlets. Heavy braids and trims beautifully complement the heavier fabrics, such as tapestries and jacquards.

Braids can also be sewn on by hand to the outside of a finished cushion. Simply unpick 5 cm in one of the side seams of your cushion cover and poke one end of the braid into the opened seam section. Then, handstitch the braid all around the cushion, poke the other end into the opening and slipstitch the opening closed.

One-colour ruffle

1 Cut the ruffle to double your chosen finished width plus 2 cm for seam allowances, and twice the circumference of your cushion cover in length. For example, for a 10 cm ruffle on a 40 cm cushion cover, your ruffle strip will measure 22 cm x 3.2 m. If necessary, join strips with a flat fell seam to achieve the required length.

2 Join the short ends of the ruffle to form a circle, again using a flat fell seam.

3 Fold the ruffle strip over double, lengthways, with the wrong sides together and the raw edges matching. Press. Gather the ruffle, 1 cm in from the raw edge with two rows of gathering stitches, either by hand or by machine.

4 To ensure that the ruffle is even all around the cushion cover, divide its length into quarters and mark these points with pins. Pull up the gathering to fit around the cushion cover front. Pin the ruffle around the right side of the cushion cover front with the right sides together and the raw edges matching, placing a pin mark at each corner of the cushion cover. Manipulate the ruffle with your fingers to place a little extra gathering at each corner for added fullness. Stitch in the line of the gathering (fig. 1).

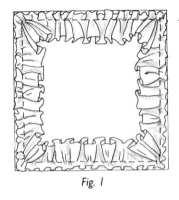

Fig. 1

5 Place the cushion cover back on top of the cushion cover front with the ruffle attached, with the right sides facing and all the raw edges matching. Baste through all thicknesses. Ensure that the ruffle is properly sandwiched between the cushion cover front and the cushion cover back, then stitch along the previous stitching line, leaving an opening for turning. Remove any visible basting stitches. Turn the cushion cover to the right side.

Two-colour ruffle

This very clever method produces a frill which works on both sides and gives the appearance of having been bound.
1 Cut two ruffle strips, one 28 cm wide and another in a contrasting fabric, 22 cm wide. The length of both strips should be twice the circumference of your cushion cover plus 3 cm for seams.
2 Place the two strips together along one long side with the right sides facing. Stitch 1 cm from the edge. Press

Ruffled cushions have an old world charm which is very appealing

the seam to one side. Join the short ends of the combined ruffle to make a circle.
3 Fold the ruffle over double, lengthways, with the wrong sides together and the raw edges matching. Press.
4 Gather both raw edges of the ruffle, 1 cm from the edge. Divide the length of the ruffle into quarters and mark these points with a pin. Draw up the ruffle to fit around the outside edge of the cushion cover front.
5 Pin the ruffle to the cushion cover front with the right sides facing and the raw edges matching, placing a pin mark at each corner. Manipulate the ruffle with your fingers to place a little extra gathering at each corner for added fullness. Stitch in the line of the gathering.
6 Place the cushion cover back on top of the cushion cover front with the ruffle attached, with the right sides facing and all the raw edges matching. Baste through all thicknesses. Ensure that the ruffle is properly sandwiched between the cushion cover front and the cushion cover back and then stitch along the previous stitching line,

leaving an opening for turning. Remove any visible basting stitches. Turn the cushion cover to the right side.

Stencilling

Stencilling was one of the first methods of printing on fabric. Pure cotton is the best choice as a fabric for stencilling. As the finish in some fabrics repels paint, wash your fabric thoroughly before applying any paint.

For cutting out a stencil, use a firm, clear plastic sheeting and cut with a scalpel or sharp craft knife.

Experiment with the stencil first on scraps of fabric to test absorption and colour strength. Don't judge a colour until it is dry. When the paint is dry, heat-seal the colours by ironing on the back of the fabric or by using a very hot hairdryer on the paint surface.

If you are repeating a pattern, for example across the top of a sheet, measure out each position before you begin stencilling. Reposition the stencil accurately each time, using masking tape to hold the stencil in place while you are working.

Mix and match cushion styles, fabric and trims to maximise the impact

Appliqué

If your machine can zigzag, you can appliqué beautiful motifs very easily.

Decide on your appliqué motif. Look for clear bunches of flowers or motifs that will be attractive as a feature.

If interfacing is necessary, cut out your fabric around the general area of the motif then, with a warm iron and a pressing cloth, fuse an equal-sized piece of interfacing to the wrong side of the fabric. Finally cut out the detail of the motif.

When using this appliqué method, choose a sewing thread close to the background colour of the fabric and always use a sharp machine needle.

Openings & closures

A cushion cover needs to be fully removable for laundering. Zippers are the most common way to close cushion covers; however, Velcro, buttons and ties are all suitable.

The placement of the opening may vary. A back vent in the middle of the back of the cushion cover is often used when the cushion does not need to be turned over. A side vent opening is concealed in a side seam so that the cushion cover can be reversible.

Decorative items, such as buttons and bows, provide added interest as well as providing a functional method for opening and closing.

Back vent opening

1 Cut the cushion cover front to the finished size plus 1.5 cm all around for seam allowances. Cut out a cushion cover back to the same size, but add 11 cm to two opposite sides to form a rectangle. Cut the rectangle in half across the long sides; these cut edges will be the centre back edges.

2 Turn in and press 1.5 cm to the wrong side along the centre back edges, then turn in and press another 1.5 cm. Stitch.

3 Place the centre back edges together so the hemmed edges overlap by 5 cm to form the back vent. Baste these edges together.

4 Complete the cushion cover as described in the instructions for the cushion you have chosen.

Velcro closure

1 Cut the cushion cover front to the finished size plus 1.5 cm seam allowances all around. Cut out a cushion cover back to the same size, but add 11 cm to two opposite sides to form a rectangle. Cut the rectangle in half across the long sides; these cut edges

will be the centre back edges.

2 Turn in and press 1.5 cm to the wrong side along the centre back edges, then turn in and press another 1.5 cm. Stitch.

3 Pin one half of the Velcro strip on to the right side of one half of the cushion cover back, over the hem just stitched. Pin the other half of the Velcro strip to the wrong side of the remaining half of the cushion cover back, over the hem just stitched. Test the closure to ensure the back will close in a perfect square before stitching the Velcro into place.

4 Complete the cushion cover as described in the instructions for the cushion you have chosen.

Buttons

1 Cut the cushion cover front to the finished size plus 1.5 cm seam allowances all around. Cut out a cushion cover back to the same size, but add 11 cm to two opposite sides to form a rectangle. Cut the rectangle in half across the long sides; these cut edges will be the centre back edges.

2 Turn in and press 1.5 cm to the wrong side along the centre back edges, then turn in and press another 1.5 cm. Stitch.

3 Mark the positions for the buttons and buttonholes on the two hems just stitched.

4 Make the buttonholes on the top half of the opening and sew the buttons to the right side of the bottom half.

5 Complete the cushion cover as described in the instructions for the cushion you have chosen.

Bows or ties

In addition to your main fabric, you will need to allow approximately 6 cm x 20 cm fabric for each tie. These can be cut on the bias or on the grain.

1 Decide how many pairs of ties you need and cut out the required pieces.

2 For each tie, fold the fabric strip over double with the right sides together and the raw edges even. Sew down the long side and one end. Turn the tie through to the right side. Press.

3 Cut out a cushion cover front and a cushion cover back with a 1.5 cm seam allowance all around. Pin the raw ends of the ties on to the right side of the cushion cover back and front, so that the raw ends of the ties match the raw edge of the cushion cover. Make sure the pairs of ties are also matching.

4 Cut two pieces of fabric for the facings, each 5 cm wide by the width of the cushion. Place one facing piece on each half of the cushion cover over the ties with the right sides facing and with the raw edge of the facing matching the raw edge of the cushion cover on the opening edge. Stitch along the opening edge. Turn the facing to the wrong side. Press.

5 Complete the cushion cover as described in the instructions for the cushion you have chosen.

Zippers

Inserting a centred zipper

1 Measure and mark on the opening the length of the zipper teeth plus 5 mm. Close the zipper seam with a basting stitch and press the seam open.

2 Open the zipper and position it face down on the seam allowance so that the zipper teeth are along the seam line. Baste the zipper into place along one side of the zipper tape. Close the zipper and baste the other side into place.

3 Turn the fabric right side up with the zipper underneath. Using the zipper foot on your sewing machine and commencing at the top of the zipper, stitch down one side, then across the bottom of the zipper and back up to the top. Remove the basting stitches.

Lapped zipper in a piped seam

1 Press the seam allowance of the opening under, along the seam line.

2 With the piped pieces together, pull back the top seam allowance to view the piping allowance.

3 Open the zipper, lay it face down over the seam allowance with the zipper teeth resting on the top of the piping. Baste along the zipper tape

Plain and printed fabrics work together well on cushions

close to the zipper teeth. Check that the zipper will open and close smoothly, before stitching it in place. Remove the basting.

Offset zipper

This method is used to conceal a zipper from view.

1 With the zipper open, position it over the opening so that the zipper teeth are centred over the right-hand seam allowance. Baste one side of the tape into position 5 mm from the zipper teeth.

2 Close the zipper and baste the other side of the zipper to the other seam allowance.

3 Turn the fabric right side up and topstitch the zipper in place through all the layers of fabric, using the zipper foot on your sewing machine and stitching close to the ends of the zipper. Remove the basting.

Top: The centred zipper

Centre: The offset zipper

Above: The zipper in the side seam

Piped Cushions

Basic piped cushion

MATERIALS

40 cm square of fabric for the cushion cover front

two pieces of fabric, each 22 cm x 40 cm, for the cushion cover backs

40 cm square cushion insert

30 cm zipper

1.7 m of corded piping (see how to make and apply piping on pages 7 and 12)

matching sewing machine thread

scissors

pins

tape measure

sewing machine

Method

1 Place the two 40 cm edges of the back pieces together with the right sides facing and the raw edges even. Stitch a 5 cm long seam at each end, leaving an opening in the centre for the zipper. Insert the zipper. Open the zipper to allow for turning the cushion cover.

2 With right sides facing and the raw edges matching, pin the piping around the edge of the cushion cover front, clipping the piping seam allowances at the corners to allow it to curve gently. Cut 2 cm of the piping cord out of one end of the piping to lessen the bulk at the overlap. Overlap the piping ends.

Sew on the piping using the zipper foot on your sewing machine and stitching as close as possible to the piping.

3 Pin and baste the cushion cover back and cushion cover front together with the right sides facing and all the raw edges matching. Stitch around all sides, stitching in the piping stitching line. Trim the seams and clip the corners.

4 Turn the cushion cover right side out through the zipper opening. Remove any basting stitches that are visible. Press.

An interesting fabric, such as this one, needs only very simple trimming to make an attractive cushion

A contrasting ruffle makes a strong decorative statement

Frilled piped cushion

MATERIALS
40 cm square of fabric for the cushion cover front

two pieces of fabric, each 22 cm x 40 cm, for the cushion cover backs

1.7 m of contrasting piping

30 cm zipper

3.2 m fabric strip for the ruffle

40 cm square cushion insert

matching sewing machine thread

scissors

pins

tape measure

sewing machine

Method

1 Make a two-colour ruffle as instructed on page 13. Make the piping as instructed on page 7 or purchase ready-made piping.

2 With the right sides of the fabric facing and the raw edges matching, sew the piping and then the completed ruffle around the edge of the cushion cover front. If you are attaching the ruffle separately, after the piping, sew in the piping stitching line.

3 Place the two 40 cm edges of the back pieces together with the right sides facing and the raw edges even. Stitch a 5 cm long seam at each end, leaving an opening in the centre for the zipper. Insert the zipper. Open the zipper to allow for turning the cushion cover to the right side.

4 Place the cushion cover back and front together with the right sides facing and the raw edges even. Sew around the outside edge following the piping stitching line. Trim the seams and clip the corners to reduce bulk. Turn the cushion cover to the right side through the zipper opening and press.

Cushion with contrast band

MATERIALS
40 cm square of fabric for the
cushion cover front

two pieces of fabric, each 22 cm x 40 cm,
for the cushion cover back

four strips of border fabric,
each 5 cm x 32 cm

1.7 m of contrasting corded piping (see
how to make corded piping on page 7)

30 cm zipper

40 cm square cushion insert

matching sewing machine thread

tape measure

scissors

pins

sewing machine

Method

1 Trim the short ends of the border strips to perfect diagonals (fig. 1). Join the strips with mitred corners to form a square (fig. 2) which fits the cushion cover, 4 cm from the outside edge, as shown. Clip in 1 cm on the inner corner seams. Press the seams open.

2 Press under 1 cm on the inside and outside edges of the square. Pin the square on to the cushion cover front. Edgestitch into place. Press.

3 Attach the piping to the cushion cover front. Insert the zipper into the cushion cover back as instructed on page 15.

Simple trimmings, cleverly applied, make a plain cushion into a unique one

4 Place the cushion cover front and cushion cover back together with the right sides facing and the raw edges matching. Stitch around the outside edge. Trim excess bulk from the corners and seams. Turn the cushion cover to the right side through the zipper opening. Press.

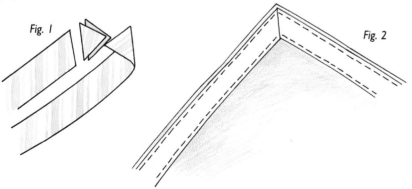

Fig. 1

Fig. 2

Machine-appliquéd cushion

MATERIALS
fabric, featuring flowers, animals,
borders or any motif that will lend
itself to being cut out

30 cm square of fabric for the
cushion cover front

two pieces of fabric, each 17 cm x 30 cm,
for the cushion cover backs

fabric strip for the ruffle, 12 cm x 2.4 m

25 cm zipper

30 cm square cushion insert

fusible interfacing (optional)

pins

scissors

matching sewing machine thread

sewing machine

warm iron

pressing cloth

Method

1 Cut out around the motif, leaving a 2 cm margin all around. Interface the motif if necessary. Pin or baste the motif on the area to be appliquéd.

2 Zigzag around the motif 5 mm in from the cut edge. Trim away the excess fabric, close to the stitching. Stitch again over the first zigzag stitching, using a slightly wider satin stitch.

3 Join the short ends of the ruffle strip. Fold the ruffle over double with wrong sides together and raw edges matching. Press. Gather the raw edges together. Apply the ruffle to the cushion front as instructed on page 12.

4 Insert the zipper into the cushion cover back as instructed on page 15, remembering to leave the zipper open.

5 Place the cushion cover back on the front, with the right sides facing. Stitch around the outside edge, through all thicknesses, following the piping stitching line. Turn the cushion cover to the right side through the zipper opening and press.

Triangular cushion

Before you begin You can make a triangular insert for this cushion from calico, following these instructions but omitting the zipper; or simply stuff the cushion cover with polyester fibre fill.

MATERIALS

60 cm of 140 cm wide fabric

2.6 m of 6 cm wide contrasting bias binding

2.6 m of piping cord

matching sewing machine thread

30 cm zipper

polyester fibre fill

scissors

pins

tape measure

sewing machine

This triangular cushion with its bright contrasting piping is the perfect foil for the checked slipcover

Method

1 Cut out two triangles with each side measuring 42 cm including a 1.5 cm seam allowance.

2 Make two lengths of piping, each one 130 cm. (See page 7.)

3 Cut a piece of fabric for the wall, 13 cm x 129 cm including seam allowances. If you need to join lengths to achieve the total length, add 1.5 cm for seam allowances on joining seams.

4 Pin the piping around the right side of the top and bottom pieces with the raw edges matching and the right sides together. Clip into the seam allowance of the piping to allow it to curve around the corners. Overlap the piping as neatly as possible at the ends, pulling the ends into the seam allowances. Stitch.

5 To attach the wall, pin and baste the ends of the strip together to form a circle. Check the fit. You may have to make a slight adjustment. Pin the wall to the top cushion piece with the right sides facing and the raw edges even. Stitch in the piping stitching line. Trim the seam allowance.

6 Stitch the wall to the bottom cushion piece in the same way as for the top, leaving a 30 cm opening along one side for the zipper. Trim any excess bulk around the corners and at the seams.

7 Insert the zipper and leave it open. (See page 15 for how to insert a zipper.) Turn the cushion to the right side through the open zipper and press.

8 Stuff the cushion firmly and evenly with the fibre fill, ensuring that the corners are well filled. Close the zipper.

Heirloom Cushions

MADE FROM SILK AND LACE, THESE CUSHIONS USE BASIC PATCHWORK
SKILLS AND HAND-APPLIQUE TO GIVE THEM A LOOK OF DISTINCTION
THAT WILL BECOME MORE CHARMING WITH AGE.

Lace patchwork cushion

MATERIALS
2 m of 5 cm wide lace
*12 cm x 192 cm of natural-coloured silk
for the cushion cover front*
*two pieces of silk, each 22 cm x 40 cm, for
the cushion cover backs*
30 cm zipper
40 cm square cushion insert
pins
needles
matching sewing machine thread
tape measure
sewing machine

Method

1 Stitch both sides of the lace down the centre of the fabric strip, stitching close to the edge of the lace. Carefully press the seams flat, then cut the strip into sixteen 12 cm squares.

2 Sew the squares together in four rows of four squares each, noting that the direction of the lace must be alternately horizontal and vertical. Sew the four rows together to form the front of the cushion cover.

3 Complete the cushion, using the cushion cover method of your choice and embellish it with your choice of trims. We have added a ruffle.

*These cushions are the
heirlooms of tomorrow*

Hand-appliquéd cushion

Before you begin The traditional hand-appliqué method is ideal for delicate voile pillowcases and lightweight cotton cushion covers, as well as chintz motifs that can be cut out and appliquéd on to softer coloured backgrounds.

MATERIALS

cushion cover of your choice

tracing paper

pencil

fabric in a contrasting colour or texture for the bow

dressmakers marker pen

needle

pins

scissors

matching sewing thread

Method

1 Trace the bow motif, using the tracing paper and pencil. Cut out the pattern pieces.

2 Pin the pattern pieces on to the right side of the cushion front and trace around each element.

3 Cut out the bow elements from the contrasting fabric, allowing an additional 5 mm around each one. Turn in and press the 5 mm allowance to the back of each piece and baste it in place. When you are working around curved shapes, gather in the basting stitch slightly so that the edge will lie flat. Snip into the corners and curves where necessary.

4 Pin the motif into position right side up and baste. Working from the back and using small slipstitches, stitch the motif in place. Remove the basting.

If you are making your own cushion cover, you can use the appliqué fabric for a ruffle or a bias trim

Stencilled Cushions

MATERIALS

firm plastic sheet for the stencil

fineline marker pen

sharp craft knife or scalpel

bread board or similar cutting board

stencil brushes

paints

masking tape

fabric for practice and testing colours

40 cm square of calico for the
cushion cover front

two pieces of calico, each 22 cm x 40 cm,
for the cushion cover back

calico strip for the ruffle

checked cotton fabric strip for
the second ruffle

40 cm square cushion insert

matching sewing machine thread

pins

scissors

tape measure

sewing machine

Method

1 Place the plastic sheet over the motif and trace around the design, using the marker pen. Cut the stencil out on the cutting board, using the sharp knife or scalpel. Remember to leave 'bridges' in the design that are not cut through.

2 Place the stencil on the cushion cover front. Define the stencil areas that will be the same colour by covering all other areas with masking tape. Taking care to paint the elements in their logical order (main colour first, then details), start stencilling from the outside, gradually filling in the entire area until you are happy with the depth of colour. Each time you finish stencilling a colour, you can cover it with tape and uncover the next area to be painted. It is a good idea to let each section of colour dry before you begin applying the next one, to avoid them bleeding into one another. Allow all the paint to dry before you begin sewing.

3 Make the two ruffles as instructed on page 12.

4 Complete the cushion in the same way as the two-colour ruffled cushion on page 13.

The stencil below provides a basic outline. Change any detail to please yourself.

For a fresh country look, stencil calico cushions with farmyard motifs

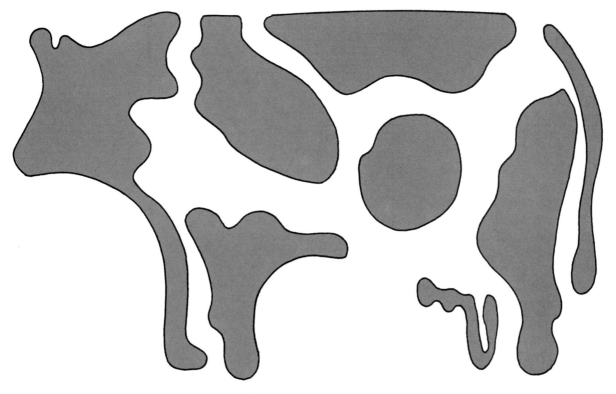

Bolsters

LARGE BOLSTERS ARE OFTEN USED AS NECK ROLLS ON A BED, WHILE SMALLER
VERSIONS ARE USED PURELY AS DECORATION FOR A WINDOW SEAT OR
TO COMPLEMENT OTHER CUSHIONS ON A LOUNGE OR A BED.

Before you begin Like cushions, bolsters can also be uniquely embellished with embroidery and a variety of trims. There are two styles of bolsters: one has a gathered end and the other has a flat end. The materials required vary slightly for the two styles.

Gathered-end bolster

MATERIALS
sufficient main fabric
bolster pad
two buttons for covering and a 5 cm square of fabric for covering each button
matching sewing machine thread
scissors
pins
tailors chalk
quilting thread
long needle
tape measure
sewing machine

Bolsters, such as these, are a charming feature on a traditional day bed

Method

1 Cut a rectangle of fabric 3 cm wider than the circumference of the bolster pad and 4.5 cm longer than the length of the bolster pad.

2 Sew the long edges together with a 1.5 cm seam and the right sides facing. Press the seam open and turn the tube right side out.

3 Position the pad in the centre of the fabric tube, so that equal amounts of fabric extend on either end. Mark the

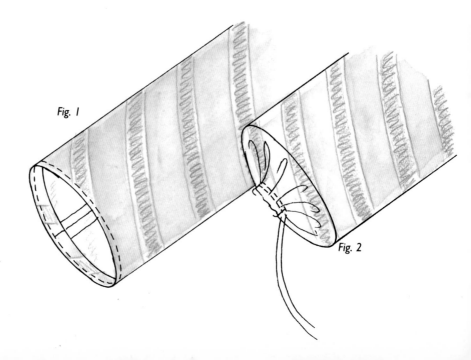

Fig. 1

Fig. 2

position of the pad with pins or chalk and remove the cover.

4 Turn in and press 1.5 cm on each end (fig. 1). Gather around the circumference of each end close to the folded edge. Replace the pad in the cover. Gather in the fabric tightly at each end and secure (fig. 2).

5 Cut out the fabric for covering the buttons, 1 cm larger than the circumference of the button. Gather around the circumference of the fabric, draw up the fabric around the button, then tie off the ends of the thread. Attach the buttons with the quilting thread and the long needle to the centre of each end, covering the gathering.

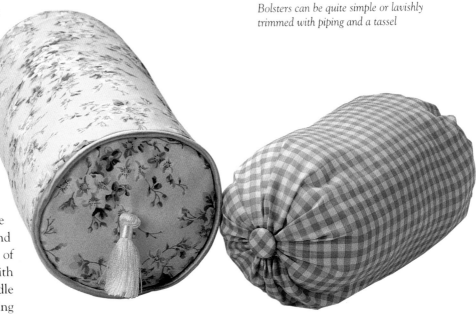

Bolsters can be quite simple or lavishly trimmed with piping and a tassel

---

Piped flat-end bolster

MATERIALS

sufficient main fabric

twice the circumference of the ends of the bolster plus 3 cm for seams in contrasting corded piping (see how to make and attach corded piping on page 7)

bolster pad

25 cm zipper

two decorative tassels

matching sewing machine thread

scissors

pins

tape measure

tailors chalk

sewing machine

Method

1 Cut a rectangle of the main fabric 3 cm longer than the bolster pad and 3 cm wider than the circumference of the pad.

2 Cut two circles for the ends of the bolster, the same diameter as the bolster pad plus 3 cm for seams.

3 Pin the piping to the right side of the fabric on the short edges of the rectangle, with the raw edges matching. Clip into the seam allowance of the piping to allow it to curve.

4 Pin the long edges of the rectangle together with the right sides facing. With a 1.5 cm seam allowance, stitch each end, leaving a 25 cm opening in the centre for the zipper. Baste the rest of the seam closed along the seam line.

5 Press the seam open. Remove the basting stitches and insert the zipper as instructed on page 15, following the method for a centred zipper (fig. 3). Undo the basting and open the zipper.

6 Cut notches into the seam allowances of the two circles. Baste the ends into place over the piping. Check that all the edges are secured in the basting, then stitch with the zipper foot on your sewing machine (fig. 4). Trim and clip the seam allowances. Turn to the right side through the zipper opening.

7 Stitch a decorative tassel into place in the centre of each end. Insert the bolster pad and close the zipper.

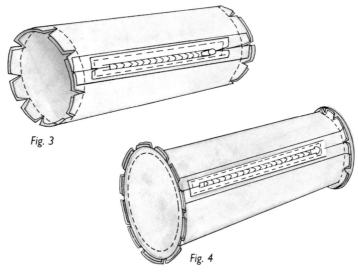

Fig. 3

Fig. 4

Chair Cushions

CHAIR CUSHIONS ARE AN EASY WAY TO ADD COMFORT AND STYLE TO
WOODEN CHAIRS. CHOOSE A WASHABLE FABRIC AND ONE THAT WILL
COMPLEMENT YOUR COLOUR SCHEME.

The shape of these two cushions will vary according to the shape of your chair, so you will need to make a pattern

Walled chair cushions

MATERIALS

*two pieces of sturdy fabric, each
45 cm x 50 cm, for the seat cushion
cover, and two pieces approximately
50 cm x 50 cm for the back rest*

*50 cm of 6 cm wide fabric strip
for the wall*

*5 m of contrasting piping (see how to make
and apply piping on pages 7 and 12)*

polyester fibre fill

large sheets of paper

pencil

ten matching covered buttons

matching sewing machine thread

tailors chalk

pins

scissors

sewing machine

Method

1 To make the pattern, trace the shape of the chair seat and the back rest on to the large sheets of paper. Following the paper pattern, cut two seat cushion pieces and two back rest pieces adding 1.5 cm seam allowance.

2 Stitch the piping around the right side of each seat cushion cover piece, clipping the seam allowance of the piping at the corners. Stitch the piping around the right side of the front of the back rest in the same way.

3 Determine where the back seam should be in the wall of the seat cushion. Starting at that point, pin the wall around the edge of one cushion cover piece, over the piping, with the right sides together and the raw edges matching. Stitch the back seam, then stitch the pinned edge of the wall to the cushion cover, following the piping stitching line.

4 With the right sides facing, pin the remaining cushion cover piece to the wall, then stitch, following the piping stitching line and leaving an opening at the back for stuffing. Turn to the right side and press. Stuff the cushion with the fibre fill, distributing the stuffing evenly.

5 Fold in the wall seam allowance at the opening. Pin it to the piping stitching line, then stitch.

6 For the back rest, place the front and back together with right sides facing and raw edges even. Stitch around the outside edge, leaving a 15 cm opening at the bottom for stuffing. Turn to the right side and press.

7 Stuff loosely. Stitch three buttons on each side, roughly corresponding to where the chair arms begin, pulling the thread firmly through the button and the stuffing to the back of the back rest. Stitch four buttons to the seat cushion in the same way.

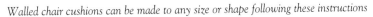

Walled chair cushions can be made to any size or shape following these instructions

Chair cushion with deep ruffle

Before you begin

You will need two fabric strips for the ruffles: one should be one and a half times the length of the back edge of the chair, the other one should be one and a half times the length of the three remaining sides of the chair allowing an extra 3 cm on each piece for hems. Decide how wide you wish your ruffle to be and add 1.5 cm for the top and bottom seam/hem allowance.

MATERIALS
two pieces of sturdy fabric, each
45 cm x 50 cm, for the cushion cover
polyester fibre fill
2 m of 6 cm wide fabric strips for ties
fabric for the ruffle strips
large sheet of paper
pencil
matching sewing machine thread
pins
scissors
tape measure
turning hook or knitting needle
sewing machine

Method

1 To make the pattern, trace the shape of the chair seat on to the large sheet of paper. Following the paper pattern, cut two cushion cover pieces.

2 To make the ruffle: Turn in and press 5 mm on the sides and ends of the two ruffle strips and then turn in and press another 5 mm. Stitch. Gather the top edge of each strip.

3 Pin and then baste the smaller ruffle to the back edge of the cushion cover front with the right sides facing and the raw edges matching, starting 2.5 cm in from both back corners. Pull up the gathering to fit. Pin and baste the longer piece around the front and side edges of the cushion cover front with the right sides facing and the raw edges matching, starting 2.5 cm in from both back corners.

4 Cut the 6 cm wide strip into four 50 cm lengths. Fold each length over double with the right sides facing and the raw edges matching. Stitch down the long side and across one short end. Turn the ties to the right side with the turning hook or knitting needle and press. Pin the ties at the four corners so that the raw edges are matching. Baste.

5 Place the cushion cover back and front together with the right sides facing and the raw edges matching and the ruffle in between. Stitch around the outside edge in the ruffle basting line, leaving an opening at the centre back.

Turn the cushion cover to the right side and press.

6 Stuff the cushion, distributing the stuffing evenly. Close the opening by hand.

Above and below: Make a ruffled chair cushion to coordinate with the blinds

Piped chair cushion

MATERIALS
*two pieces of sturdy fabric, each
45 cm x 50 cm, for the cushion cover*

polyester fibre fill

*1.5 m of corded piping (see how to make
and apply corded piping on pages 7 and 12)*

2 m of 14 cm wide fabric strips for ties

large sheet of paper

pencil

matching sewing machine thread

pins

scissors

tape measure

turning hook or knitting needle

sewing machine

Method

1 To make the pattern, trace the shape of the chair seat on to the large sheet of paper. Following the paper pattern, cut two cushion cover pieces.

2 Apply the corded piping to the right side of one cushion piece.

3 Cut the 14 cm wide strip of fabric into four 50 cm lengths. Fold each length over double with the right sides facing and the raw edges matching.

A cushion adds comfort as well as charm to a wooden chair

Stitch down the long side and across one short end. Turn the ties to the right side with the turning hook or knitting needle and press. Place the ties on the right side of the front cushion cover, matching the raw edges. Baste.

4 Place the cushion cover back and front together with the right sides facing and the raw edges matching. Stitch around the outside edge in the piping stitching line, leaving an opening for stuffing at the centre back. Turn the cushion cover to the right side. Press.

5 Stitch around four little squares evenly spaced in the centre of the cushion (fig. 1). Stuff the cushion with the fibre fill, distributing the stuffing evenly. Close the opening by hand.

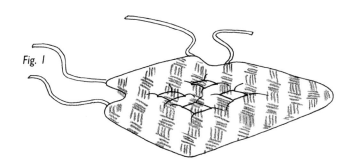

Fig. 1

Round Buttoned Cushion

MATERIALS

1 m of 120 cm wide fabric plus fabric
to cover the buttons (approximately
10 cm square for each button)

2.4 m of corded piping (see how to make
corded piping on page 7)

two buttons

matching sewing machine thread

quilting thread

quilting needle

polyester fibre fill

pins

tape measure

scissors

sewing machine

brown paper

pencil

string

thumb tack

dressmakers cutting board

Method

1 To make a paper pattern for the circles, cut a square of brown paper larger than the area of your cushion, then fold the paper into quarters so that the folded centre of the paper is at the upper left corner. With the thumb tack, pin the piece of string to the corner at the folded centre, pushing the thumb tack through into the cutting board underneath. Tie the pencil to the other end of the string at a distance equal to the radius of the circle required. (The radius is the distance from the centre of a circle to its circumference.) In the cushion shown here the radius is 20 cm. Draw the quarter of the circle on the paper and cut along the drawn line through all the thicknesses of paper. Unfold the paper and you should have a perfect circle of the size you need (figs 1 and 2).

2 Trace the circle pattern on to your fabric to give you two equal circles.

3 Sew the piping around the right sides of the front and back of the cushion cover with right sides together and raw edges matching, clipping into the seam allowance of the piping to allow it to curve.

4 Cut a strip of fabric, 10 cm x 1.26 m, for the cushion wall.

5 If it is necessary to join fabric for the wall strip, ensure that all pieces are cut in the same direction on the fabric with the grain running in the same direction. Join the pieces into a circle with flat fell seams and trim away any excess fabric. Press the seam open.

6 With the right sides together, pin one edge of the wall to the cushion cover front, sandwiching the piping in between, and stitch it into place through all thicknesses. Trim the excess fabric, clip into the curve all the way around and press the seam open.

7 Pin and stitch the other edge of the wall to the back of the cushion cover as for the front, leaving an opening for turning. Trim the seam as for the front and press the seam open.

8 Turn the cushion cover right side out. Insert the filling and slipstitch the opening closed.

9 Cut out the fabric for covering the buttons, 1 cm larger than the circumference of the button. Gather around the circumference of the fabric, draw up the fabric around the button, then tie off the ends of the thread.

10 With the quilting thread and the quilting needle, attach one button to the cushion front and one button to the cushion back, drawing the needle through the cushion cover at least three times from button to button to ensure they are securely attached.

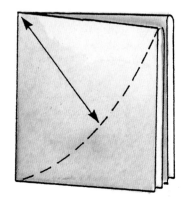

Fig. 1

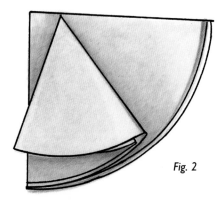

Fig. 2

A pretty brocade works very well for this style of cushion

New Covers

EDGE TREATMENTS
ARMCHAIR COVER
DIRECTORS CHAIRS
TAILORED CHAIR COVER
RUFFLED CHAIR COVER
INSTANT SOFA COVER-UP

New Covers

IT IS USUALLY BEST TO LEAVE TRADITIONAL UPHOLSTERY TO THE PROFESSIONALS, BUT THERE ARE LOTS OF QUICK AND EASY FURNITURE-COVERING PROJECTS SUITABLE FOR THE ENTHUSIAST.

Wouldn't that old sofa that you bought at the last jumble sale look great with a smart new cover? A few metres of fabric and a couple of weekends' work and hey presto, a new sofa! If only it were that easy. Traditional furniture upholstery can be a minefield of pitfalls for the amateur. Furnishing fabrics are expensive and mistakes can quickly swallow up your decorating budget. Even the simplest type of upholstery involves fixing a covering fabric over a tightly stretched calico cover which itself covers padding of some kind and possibly springs. The variety of furniture shapes and styles is almost endless. Some furniture pieces have shapes which create particular problems and awkward corners to work around.

There are very simple cover projects – such as renewing dining-room chairs, or recovering cushions –

that are perfect 'Do It Yourself' projects. There are step-by-step instructions for these in the following pages. These projects are not 'upholstery' in the traditional sense – no repairs, new stuffing, webbing or springs are required. They do, however, provide decorative solutions to tired and worn-out chairs, or practical removable covers where laundering is required.

Choosing fabric

Choosing the right fabric for the job and the room is crucial to the success of the project, but the great variety of fabrics available can be daunting for the home decorator. The four natural fibres – cotton, wool, silk and linen – are widely used in upholstery. Cotton, which is mass-produced and generally economical, is a popular choice for slipcovers and cushions. Prewash all cottons to allow any shrinkage to take place before cutting out your pattern. Wool is very hard-wearing, flame-resistant, light and relatively waterproof. It has been popular for furniture coverings from time to time. Silk is the glamour fabric, but because of its relatively high cost is usually reserved for trimming, cushions or luxury pieces. Linen is one of the oldest domestic fibres and because of its long-wearing qualities has always been a popular choice for loose covers – especially in high-traffic areas. Many synthetic fibres are also available these days and are often blended with natural fibres. This reduces fabric cost and takes advantage of the good wearing and washing qualities of polyester and viscose.

Colour and pattern

The choice of colour and pattern for a particular loose cover or upholstery project will be determined by a number of factors. Are you re-covering an entire suite or will your new cover have to fit in with existing pieces? Is your room big enough to cope with that large splashy floral or will your print be overwhelmed by other objects in the room? Do you need to warm up a room with yellows, pinks and reds or do you need to cool it down with blue? Remember that colours can be very affected by the light in a room, both natural and artificial. Working with a story board of the total room colour and pattern concept will be a big help. Before buying metres of fabric, it is a good idea to take home a large sample piece. Drape it over your sofa or chair and leave it there for a day or two so you can judge the effect of the light in the room and how you think it will fit in with the curtains, wallpaper and other colours and patterns in the room. Generally, the larger your room the more you can get away with. There are exceptions, of course, but as a rule of thumb, it will help you avoid decorating disasters.

Matching patterns, where fabric pieces join in upholstery can be a nightmare. If you are not experienced, or endowed with the patience of Job, you are probably best to stick to plains or all-over small prints which do not need matching. Stripes do need careful matching but provide their own easy-to-follow guidelines. Floral bouquets or medallion patterns are more difficult because the motif has to be centred on seats cushions and backs, wasting a lot of fabric. Checks are the hardest of all, having to be matched in all directions at once.

Before you buy, it's a good idea to assess whether the fabric you like will present pattern-matching problems. Lay two lengths side by side as though they were joined, then move one slightly up or down. Now stand back and see the difference. You can do the same test if patterns are to meet end to end.

Trimming

❖

Piping and trims add the finishing professional touch to your coverings. They also define the line of a piece of furniture and give strength to areas, such as the arms, that receive constant hard wear. When selecting a suitable colour for piping or trims, it is usual to highlight one of the colours used in small amounts found in your fabric. If you use one of the colours from the main colour palette of your fabric the piping will blend in rather than create a decorative highlight.

There are different gauges of piping cord available and the size you should select is determined by the fabric to which it will be attached. As a general rule, a thick fabric requires a thin cord and a thin or fine fabric will require a thicker gauge cord to give the fabric body. Upholstery piping is often called 'welting'; this is simply a trade name for the same product.

On page 12, you will see how to make piping for cushions. The same method can be applied to upholstery piping. Lengths of bias fabric are joined with 5 mm seams, or you can cut continuous bias (see page 7). Lay the piping cord on the wrong side of the fabric. To join the ends of the piping cord, butt the ends together and bind them neatly with a heavy embroidery thread. Fold the fabric in half, enclosing the cord. Stitch close to the cord, using the zipper foot on your sewing machine.

Edge Treatments

CHOOSING THE RIGHT EDGE TREATMENT FOR THE BOTTOM OF YOUR LOOSE
COVERS IS A MATTER OF PERSONAL TASTE AND STYLE.

Before you begin
A frilled or ruffled edge creates a look of cottage comfort, informal yet inviting; knife pleats ensure a tailored look; soft scalloped edges are harmonious and feminine; while a flush edge gives a neat and simple finish. Concealed edges show the clean lines of the chair or suite, enhancing the natural characteristics of the fabric. Braids can be used to cover seam lines and can be secured with upholstery tacks.

A staple gun is a handy tool for securing fabrics on to a wooden base. The staples can subsequently be covered with flat braids.

Concealed bottom edge

Before you begin
This method will give you a fitted tailored look with four separate flaps (one for each side of the base) that are secured underneath the chair with ties.

You will need four 12 cm wide strips: two that are the same length as the width of the chair base and two that are the same length as the depth of the chair base. Add 5 cm to the length of each flap for the side hems and 2.5 cm for the bottom hem.

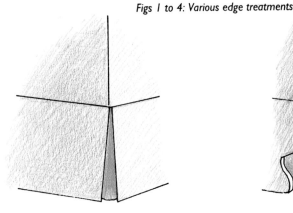
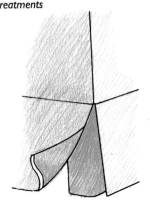

Figs 1 to 4: Various edge treatments

MATERIALS
four fabric flaps, the same as the body fabric of the chair cover
sewing machine with a needle suitable for sewing through several layers of fabric
gauge 4 cord
large safety pin
pins
scissors
tape measure

Method

1 Pin the flaps to the bottom edges of the chair cover. Trim away the excess fabric around the chair legs or castors, leaving at least a 2.5 cm seam allowance. Remove the flaps. Turn in and press 5 mm on the side edges, then turn in and press another 2 cm. Machine-stitch the side hems in place.

2 Turn in and press 5 mm along the raw bottom edges of the flaps, then turn in and press another 2 cm. Stitch the bottom hems in place, forming a casing by stitching close to both folds. Stitch the flaps to the chair cover.

3 Using the safety pin, thread the cord loosely through the casing. Fit the cover over the chair. Turning the chair on its side, pull up the cord and tie the two ends of the cord in a bow or knot (fig. 5).

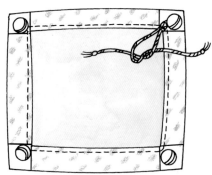

Fig. 5

Ruffled valance

Before you begin

Measure around the bottom edge of the chair cover. For the ruffles, you will need twice this measurement plus 1.5 cm for each seam allowance on any joining seams. Determine the depth of the valance by measuring from the bottom edge of the cover to 1 cm above the floor. Add 2.5 cm for the hem and another 1.5 cm for the gathering and top seam allowance.

MATERIALS

fabric, the same as the body fabric of the cover

sewing machine with a needle suitable for sewing through several layers of fabric

matching sewing machine thread

quilting thread for gathering up the ruffle (optional)

pins

scissors

tape measure

Method

1 Cut as many strips of the required depth as you need to achieve the total length, following the grainline of the fabric and matching the pattern. Join the strips together into a long strip with flat fell seams.

2 Hem the bottom edge and the short ends by machine or by hand; the latter method is preferable if a light fabric is being used, so that the stitches are not obvious.

3 Gather along the top edge and pull up the gathers to fit the bottom of the chair cover. With the right sides together, pin and baste the frill to the bottom edge of the chair cover, allowing extra fullness at the corners. Place the cover on the chair and make any final adjustments before machine-stitching the valance into place, placing the opening at the back leg, where the chair cover is also open.

❖

Box-pleated valance

Before you begin

The valance must begin and end at the back leg where the chair cover is also open. The pleats should be evenly arranged, preferably with a pleat at each corner, one at the centre front and one at the centre back. Making a newspaper pattern like the ones here is a good idea (figs 6 and 7).

Measure around the bottom edge of the cover. You will need three times this measurement plus 1.5 cm for each seam allowance on any joining seams. Determine the height of the pleat by measuring from the bottom edge of the cover to 1 cm above the floor. Add 2.5 cm for the hem and another 1.5 cm for the top seam allowance.

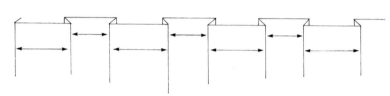

Fig 7: Measure around the bottom of the chair and determine the width of each pleat

MATERIALS

fabric, the same as the body fabric of the chair cover

sewing machine with a needle suitable for sewing through several layers of fabric

matching sewing machine thread

stiff cardboard, the width of your pleat by the final depth of the box-pleated edge

tailors chalk

pins

scissors

pencil

steel ruler

Method

1 Cut as many strips of the required size as you need to achieve the total length, following the grainline of the fabric. Join the strips together into one long strip with flat fell seams.

2 Hem the bottom edge and the two short ends.

3 Cut a cardboard template for the pleats, the width of your pleat (say 20 cm) x the height of the pleat. Moving the template along the length of the fabric, mark the pleats with tailors chalk, marking both the top and bottom edges as shown in the diagram.

4 Fold and pin the pleats, then baste them in place. Press the pleats carefully. Machine-stitch across the top to secure the pleats. Remove the basting.

5 To attach the valance, begin at the back leg where the cover is open and pin the valance to the bottom edge of the chair cover, with the right sides together and the raw edges even. Stitch.

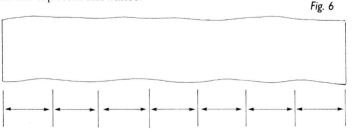

Fig. 6

Armchair Cover

YOU MAY NOT BE ABLE TO RUN UP A NEW ARMCHAIR ON YOUR SEWING
MACHINE, BUT YOU CAN CERTAINLY GIVE THE OLD ONE A TOTALLY FRESH
LOOK WITH NEW FABRIC AND A LITTLE INGENUITY!

Before you begin Easy covering is all about revamping furniture with minimum fuss and expense. If the frame of your chair is solid, but the fabric is shabby, this type of re-covering is an ideal solution for the home sewer. However, if your chair has stretched, or torn webbing or the odd spring is poking through, a 'bandaid solution' is not enough – you will have to consider using a professional upholsterer.

The instructions given here are for re-covering an armchair, but you can cover a settee in exactly the same way.

Measuring

Measuring and making a pattern for your loose chair or sofa cover is an exacting process. When you are making a large investment in fabric, it is essential that you buy the correct quantity. Remember, it is a good form of insurance to buy an extra 50 cm of fabric. If it is not needed for the cover,

it could be converted into a beautiful throw cushion to complement your loose cover. Time is your best friend when measuring for loose covers – avoid working in a hurry and always recheck all measurements. It is often wise when making a loose cover to make a calico pattern or mock-up first so that any problems or adjustments can be made at this preliminary stage rather than

with your expensive fabric.

Make a sketch or drawing of the piece you are covering, with the measurements for each plane of the chair marked on it (fig. 1). On this same piece of paper keep a running list of all measurements. This list should include measurements for: inside back, seat, inside arms, outside arms, front border, front scrolls, back scrolls, outside back,

Fig. 1

Fig. 2

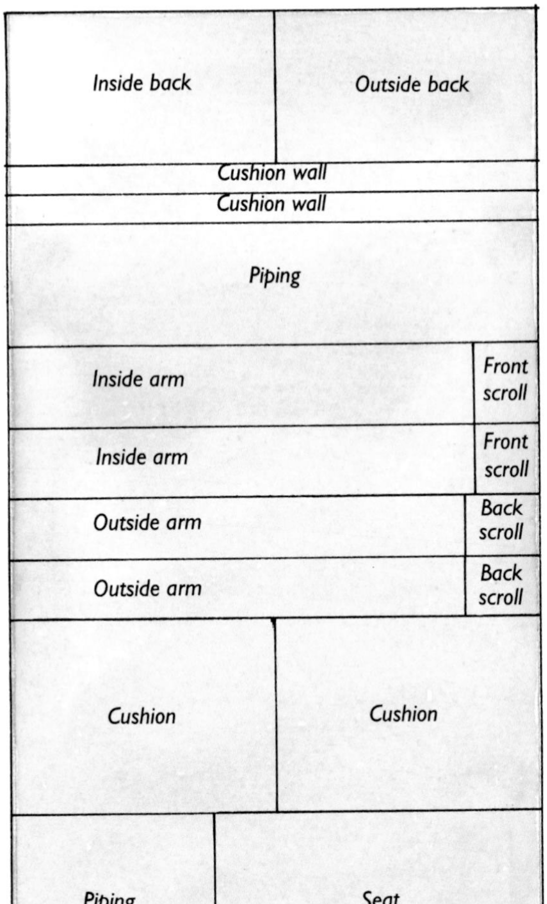

Inside back		Outside back	
Cushion wall			
Cushion wall			
Piping			
Inside arm			Front scroll
Inside arm			Front scroll
Outside arm			Back scroll
Outside arm			Back scroll
Cushion		Cushion	
Piping		Seat	

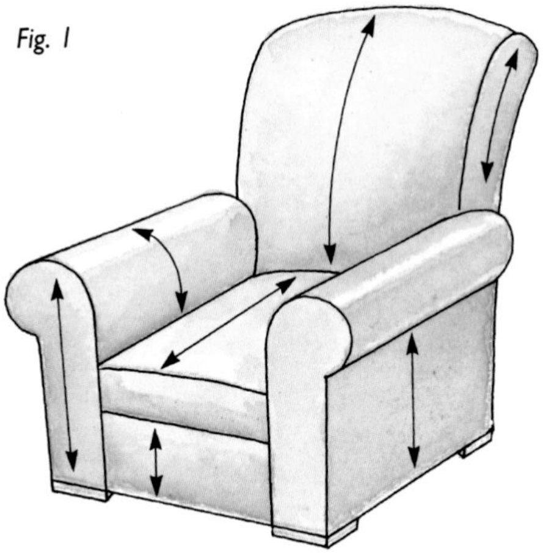

cushion, cushion borders and piping. Always write the measurements with the length of the fabric shown first, followed by the width. The drawing and the list will prove a handy cross-check system for all your measurement requirements.

Consider the style of the furniture piece as well as the pattern and weave of the fabric. When working with a patterned fabric, the pattern on the arms of the chair should run in line with the centre back, which should in turn be in line with the seat. When working with a fabric that has a raised pile, the pile must always run down the chair. Always take measurements on the widest point of each section and allow 2.5 cm for each seam allowance. Add an additional 10 cm for the tuck-in, the part of the fabric that runs between the seat and the inside back and helps to keep the cover in place.

If the chair has a removable cushion, remember to take the cushion out so that you can measure the cover that sits underneath it. You will also need to decide how you wish to finish the bottom edge of your covers. On pages 36 to 37, you will see a number of options. Allow extra fabric for whichever of these options you choose.

Also, remember to allow fabric for piping. Approximately 6.5 m of piping can be made from 25 cm of 122 cm wide fabric. It is a good idea to allow enough fabric for covers for arm rests or head rests, which will help to protect your chairs from soiling.

When cutting out your pattern, work with rectangles of fabric that are a little larger than you need. They can be trimmed to shape and size as you go.

Linens and cottons should always be cut with pinking shears in order to minimise fraying.

Pattern layout (fig. 2)
To calculate your fabric requirements, draw up a scaled pattern with each separate pattern piece drawn in and its correct positioning (in relation to the

Contrasting piping is a feature of this charming floral armchair slipcover

grain and pattern of the fabric) noted. Where pieces are required that are larger than the width of the fabric, for example on the inside back – try to get the best possible pattern placement. If this is impossible, join two pieces together with a piped seam to disguise the imperfect match.

MATERIALS
sufficient calico, approximately 8 m for an armchair

upholstery weight fabric, the same quantity as the calico, allowing extra for pattern matching (2 to 5 m additional fabric)

upholstery pins or upholstery tape

tailors chalk or masking tape for marking pieces

quilting thread

matching sewing machine thread

upholstery needle

Velcro tape or hook-and-eye tape

felt tip marker pen

sewing machine with a suitable upholstery-gauge needle

sufficient bias-cut fabric strips (the width of the strips will be determined by the gauge of the cord used)

sufficient suitable-gauge piping cord

Method

1 Cut rectangles from the calico for each piece marked on your pattern layout. With the felt tip pen, mark the location of each pattern piece on the calico.

2 Working with one piece at a time, pin with upholstery pins or tape each calico piece to the area to which it belongs. Mark the final shape on each piece. Remove the calico pieces and adjust each shape with a 2.5 cm seam allowance all around. Place each piece back in position to check the fit.

3 Pin all the pieces together.

4 Sewing pieces together in the right order will help to ensure that the finished pattern can be easily worked. Baste with the quilting thread in the following order:

- the outer back piece to the inside back;
- the inside back to the seat;
- the seat to the lower front panel;
- the seat to the arms along the inside edge;
- the inside arm to the outside arm;
- the front of the arms between the inner and outer arms;
- the end of the arm pieces to the back and inside back, leaving an opening on one back seam approximately 35 cm from the base to the back of the inside scroll; and
- the bottom edge treatment.

5 Slip the cover on the chair, inside out. On curved areas, such as the arms, it may now be necessary to take out some fullness. Do this by unpicking the basting stitches and making tiny gathers or pleats on the wrong side, taking up the slack. Make any darts as necessary. Stitch the basting back into place again to ensure a perfect fit. Once you are satisfied with the fit of the pattern, remove it from the chair. Cut through all the basting stitches, making tailors

tacking marks. Highlight all seam lines, gathering and darts with tailors chalk.

6 Lay the fabric on the floor with the right side facing up. Place the calico pattern pieces (right side up) on top of the fabric, checking that the grain is running in the correct direction. Mark out and label the fabric pieces, marking the top and bottom of each piece. Once all the pieces are marked they can be cut out.

7 If you are going to use piping, make up sufficient piping, allowing a little extra. Apply the piping to the right side of all pieces to be piped, with right sides together and raw edges matching. (See pages 7 and 12 for how to apply piping.)

8 Follow the same method for joining pieces as you did with the calico pattern, inserting the piping between the fabric layers as you work through each section.

9 Machine-stitch one half of the Velcro tape to each side of the back opening (fig. 1). Zippers are not recommended because they are often not strong enough, but hooks and eyes, spaced evenly along the opening, can be used.

10 If you wish to add a box-pleated valance like the one pictured, follow the instructions on page 37.

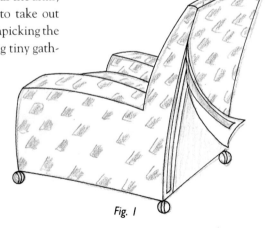

Fig. 1

Sewing corners

Shaping around curved backs or arms is possible in a number of ways:

- Handsew gathering stitches along the seam line on the curve. Pull up the gathering to fit and join the pieces together (fig. 2).
- Making small flat pleats is another way to achieve a smooth finish (fig. 3).
- If there is a lot of fullness to be taken out, darts are a good method to consider. Pin the darts as shown to confirm a good fit, before you stitch (fig. 4).
- If your chair back has straight corners, join the pieces as shown in fig. 5.

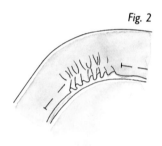

Fig. 2

Fig. 3

Fig. 4

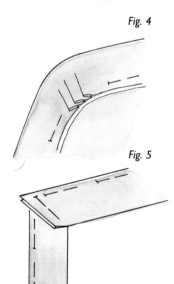

Fig. 5

Walled seat cushion

Before you begin

Loose, walled seat cushions are often found on sofas and lounge suites. The method given here is a basic guide for covering a foam block cushion.

The same method can be used for other fillings such as down and feather or foam chips, but a tightly woven cover from calico or cotton should be made first to hold the filling in place.

For most upholstery-weight cushions, it is best to conceal the zipper in the side seam so that the cushion can be reversed to share the wear and tear.

MATERIALS
fabric, the same as the main chair fabric
contrasting fabric for piping
suitable-gauge piping cord
upholstery thread
upholstery needle
sewing machine with a needle suitable for sewing through several layers of fabric
30 to 40 cm metal zipper (depending on the size of the cushion)
tailors chalk

Method

1 Cut two pieces of fabric large enough to cover the top and bottom of the cushion pad with 2.5 cm seam allowances all around.

bias strips from the contrasting fabric to achieve that length and wide enough to wrap around the piping cord you have chosen plus 1 cm on each side for seam allowances. Make the piping and join the lengths as shown on page 12.

3 Pin the piping to the right side of the top and bottom panels with the raw edges matching and right sides together. Cut a square from the seam allowance of the piping to allow it to curve around the corners (fig. 6). Where the two ends of the piping meet, cross them over as neatly as possible, pulling the ends into the seam allowances. Stitch.

4 For the wall of the cushion cover, cut four strips to the required length, allowing a 2.5 cm seam allowance at each end of each one. With the right sides facing, pin and baste all the short

ends together, forming a square (fig. 7). This is a good time to check the fit. Stitch and press the seams open.

5 Stitch the bottom panel to the wall, with right sides facing and raw edges even, stitching over the piping stitching line.

6 Insert the zipper between one side wall and the top panel. (See page 15 for how to insert the zipper.)

7 Pin and baste the top panel to the remaining three walls in the same way as for the bottom panel. Try the cushion cover on the pad to check the fit, then stitch the seams. Turn the cover through to the right side through the open zipper. Press.

Most sofas and armchairs have loose seat cushions

Fig. 6

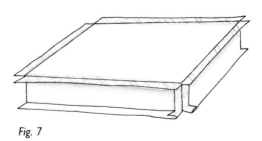

Fig. 7

Directors Chairs

Before you begin
Starting at the front of your chair at ground level, measure the distance up to the seat plus the depth of the seat up to the top of the chair back plus the distance from the top of the chair, then back to ground level. Record the measurement for the depth of the seat and the width of the back rest separately. Measure from the ground level up to and over each arm rest down to the seat. Add 1.5 cm seam allowances to all measurements. Make rough drawings, marking in these measurements.

MATERIALS
pencil and paper
approximately 2.8 m of 120 cm wide fabric
30 cm of contrasting fabric for the ties
matching sewing machine thread
scissors
tape measure
pins
sewing machine

Method 1

1 Using your drawings as a guide, cut out the three pattern pieces. Cut four 15 cm wide ties, each 40 cm long.
2 Do not remove the existing seat or back rest; the slipcover will slip over the top. Place the main pattern piece over the chair, face downwards. Do the same with each arm piece. Pin the arm pieces to the main piece at the seat level and at the front leg. Pin the front and back of the main piece together down to the arm level of the chair, finishing pinning at this point.
3 At the front of the chair, pin a dart across the top of each arm front at right angles to the front seam to ensure the drape over the arm sits straight.
4 Remove the slipcover and machine-

stitch all the seams into place. Trim the excess seam allowance, if necessary.
5 Return the slipcover to the chair (still inside out). Turn in 5 mm, then turn another 1 cm for the hem around the bottom of the slipcover and at the openings at the back legs.
6 Fold the strip for each tie over double with the right sides together and the raw edges even. Sew one short end and the long side. Turn through to the right side. Pin and baste the raw end

of one tie to the hem on the front and back edges of each back opening. Remove the slipcover from the chair and stitch all the hems and seams, catching the ties as you go. Turn the slipcover to the right side and press.

Below: A bold check cotton slipcover gives new life to an old chair
Right: The painted chair frame and the combination of many coordinating fabrics give this setting a decorator's touch

Method 2

Before you begin Applying two coats of high gloss enamel paint will give the frame an instant lift. Sand lightly between coats to give a satin-smooth finish.

If you are working with a heavy sateen or upholstery fabric, use a double thickness of fabric for extra strength. Fusible webbing between the layers of fabric will also add strength and keep the fabrics firmly in place.

Measuring

Measure from the top of the back rest down to the seat and along the seat to the front of the chair. This measurement plus the allowances for turnings at both ends is the total length. Measure the width required and add sufficient length to fold the fabric around the frame on both sides.

On a large sheet of paper, draw a rectangle to the length and width you have calculated. At one end of the rectangle mark the length of the back rest. At the other end, mark the depth of the seat. Do not forget to add sufficient allowance for turnings.

Draw in the shape of the chair cover with a rectangle at one end for the back rest and one rectangle at the other end for the seat, connected by a curved back rest extension.

MATERIALS
large sheet of paper
pencil
ruler
high gloss enamel paint
paintbrush
sufficient fabric
fusible webbing
heavy-gauge sewing machine needle
matching sewing machine thread
pins
heavy duty staples and stapler
scissors
tape measure
sewing machine

Method

1 Remove the existing covers and paint the wooden frame.
2 Cut out the fabric (or fabrics) for the chair cover. If you are using two fabrics, fuse them together with the fusible webbing. Turn in and stitch a double hem at each end of the fabric.
3 Make a narrow double hem along both sides of the fabric.
4 Place the cover on the chair, taking the turnings over to the wrong side, then attaching the cover to the frame with heavy duty staples.

Tailored Chair Cover

IF YOU HAVE WOODEN DINING CHAIRS THAT ARE STILL SOLID BUT HAVE SEEN BETTER DAYS, THIS SLIPCOVER PROJECT IS AN IDEAL REFURBISHING SOLUTION.

Before you begin This easy-cover project may be the perfect opportunity to convert six odd chairs into a matched set. This slipcover pattern is designed for chairs which are flat across the top of the back rest and do not have protruding knobs – all the lines and surfaces of the chair should be as straight as possible. Bowed backs and curved seats will not allow the fabric to hang properly. Choose your fabric carefully. You will need a sturdy material that doesn't present too many problems with matching patterns on adjacent surfaces.

Choose a contrasting or complementary fabric for the lining as it is sure to show at the joins. If you like, the slipcover can be lined with the main fabric for an all-over look.

For added comfort you can include a layer of wadding between the main fabric and the lining.

Measuring
You will need to take the measurements of your own chair then draw those rectangles on to a sheet of paper. Mark each rectangle with its position and mark all the measurements on it. The drawings here are intended as a guide only.

• *Pattern piece 1* Measure the length from the seat up the chair back and down to the floor (allowing for the width of the chair frame at the top of the back rest) by the width of the chair (allowing for the width of the chair frame at the sides).

• *Pattern piece 2* Measure the depth of the seat plus the distance to the floor by the width of the chair.

• *Pattern piece 3* Measure the depth of the seat plus the width of the timber frame by the height of the seat from the floor. Cut two.

Once you have established these measurements you can calculate the amount of fabric required.

MATERIALS
sheet of paper
pencil
ruler
main fabric
lining fabric
wadding in the same size (optional)
matching sewing machine thread
pins
scissors
tape measure
sewing machine

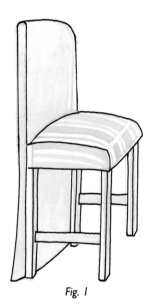

Fig. 1

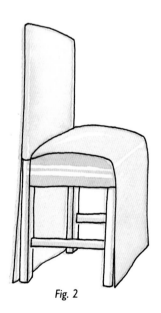

Fig. 2

Fig. 3

Method

1 Cut out the pattern pieces from the main and the lining fabric, allowing 1.5 cm all around for seams. Take care to match and centre any fabric pattern at this point.

2 On pattern piece 1, sew the sides together from the top of the chair back rest to the seat (fig. 1). Press.

3 Sew pattern piece 1 to pattern piece 2 at the seat back edge (fig. 2). Attach a pattern piece 3 at each side (fig. 3). Press.

4 Make eight 30 cm long ties out of scraps of the cover fabric. Pin one end of each tie, with the raw edges matching, on the right side of the fabric front and back edges, just below seat height.

5 Make the lining in the same way as for the cover. Place the lining and the cover together with the right sides facing and the raw edges even. Sew around the outside edge, leaving an opening for turning, and catching the ends of the ties in the seam. Turn the cover right side out, taking care to push the corners out completely. Press.

Match up your odd chairs with a set of tailored slipcovers like this

Ruffled Chair Cover

A LOOSE COVER FOR A CHAIR WITHOUT ARMS IS EASY TO MAKE AND OFFERS A
SOLUTION TO SEASONAL DECORATING WITHOUT MAJOR COST.

Ruffles and swags make a charming dining setting. See page 56 for how to make the tablecloth

Before you begin If you are new to making slipcovers, it is best to use a plain fabric or one with a small all-over print that does not need to be pattern matched. Remember, if you are working with floral bouquets or a medallion print, centre the pattern on the front of the chair back and on the seat.

Measuring

Measure the various planes of the chair (such as the width and depth of the back rest and seat, and the height of the seat from the floor) and mark these measurements on a sketch pattern of your chair.

MATERIALS
sufficient fabric (we used approximately 4 m for our chair, allowing for the fullness in the skirt)
paper and pencil
10 cm Velcro tape
pins
scissors
tape measure
tailors chalk
matching sewing machine thread
sewing machine

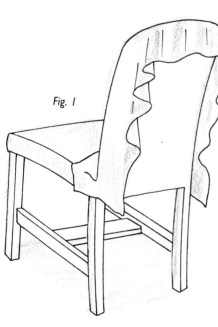

Fig. 1

Method

1 Cut out a rectangle of fabric each for the chair seat, the front of the back rest and the back of the back rest, using the measurements on your sketch pattern and following the grainlines of the fabric. Cut out the skirt to the length required plus 3 cm for the hem and one and a half times the distance around the chair seat. If necessary, join pieces with a flat fell seam to achieve the required length. Add 1.5 cm for each seam allowance. Make sure all the prints match up.

Fig. 2

2 Place the piece for the front of the back rest on the chair with the wrong side facing out (figs 1 and 2). Check the fit. If there is excess fabric bulk, you can pin darts or gather the edge to make the fabric sit more neatly. (See page 40 for how to deal with corners.) Treat the piece for the back of the back rest in the same way as the front.

3 While the pieces are still on the chair, pin the outer and inner back rest pieces together with wrong sides facing out. Check the fit and re-pin the darts if necessary. Mark the seam lines with tailors chalk. Remove the back rest pieces from the chair.

4 Stitch around the top and sides,

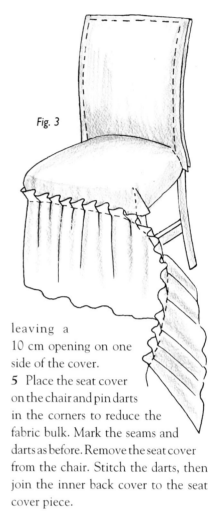

Fig. 3

leaving a 10 cm opening on one side of the cover.

5 Place the seat cover on the chair and pin darts in the corners to reduce the fabric bulk. Mark the seams and darts as before. Remove the seat cover from the chair. Stitch the darts, then join the inner back cover to the seat cover piece.

6 Turn in and press 5 mm on the bottom and the ends of the skirt, then turn in and press another 2.5 cm. Stitch the hems in place. Divide the top edge of the skirt into quarters and mark these points with a pin. Gather the top edge of the skirt.

7 Pin the skirt to the seat cover with the right sides together and the raw edges matching, beginning and ending at one of the back corners (fig. 3). Pull up the gathering to fit, placing a pin mark at each corner. Adjust the gathering, making it a little fuller at the corners. Stitch the skirt into place. Press.

8 Sew Velcro to the back opening to close the cover or make ties from scraps of fabric and sew them to either side of the opening.

9 If you wish to create a very charming effect, make two bows from the same fabric and slipstitch one to each side of the chair.

Instant Sofa Cover-up

INSTANT LOOSE COVERS REQUIRE LITTLE SEWING, ONLY A SMALL FINANCIAL
INVESTMENT AND NOT A LOT OF TIME.

Before you begin

Practise your skills by draping an old sheet on your chair or sofa. This way you will quickly be able to work out where fabric can be tucked into crevices to anchor it. If the existing sofa has torn covers and you are not likely to use it again in its present state, sew strips of Velcro to the old lounge to marry up with Velcro on the fabric cover. The Velcro will help the fabric to stay neatly in position and it will not crease as much.

Select a fabric, such as a linen or another woven fabric, that is less likely to show creases. Fabric bows on the arms add a further decorative touch and can be attached with Velcro, stitched or pinned into place.

You should use 137 cm wide fabric for a two-seater sofa, as fewer joins will be necessary.

MATERIALS

fabric

pins

tailors chalk

Velcro (if required)

cord, ribbon or sewn ties

Method

1 It may be necessary to join lengths of fabric together to achieve the required width. If this is the case, use flat fell seams for added strength and always carefully match the fabric pattern.

2 Remove the seat cushions. Drape and tuck the fabric piece over the base of the lounge. When you are happy with the draping, mark the hem line with tailors chalk. Remove the cover. Even out any great irregularities in the chalk marks, then trim the excess fabric from the hem. Turn in and press a double hem. Stitch the hem in place.

3 Tie sashes, ribbons or cords around the arms to hold the fabric in place. The ties can be attached with Velcro, pins or by topstitching them into place.

Pleat the fabric at the arms for a neat finish

Wrapped seat cushion

MATERIALS
sufficient fabric
pinking shears
safety pins (optional)
needle and thread (optional)

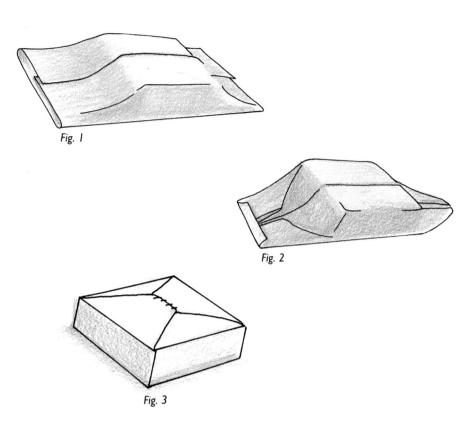

Fig. 1

Fig. 2

Fig. 3

Method

1 Use pinking sheers to cut out a fabric square twice the width and length of your cushion plus 30 cm. Place the cushion in the centre of the fabric, on the wrong side.

2 Wrap the cushion as if it were a present; first fold the fabric to the centre, turning in the raw edges. Secure the fabric on the underside with safety pins or stitches. Place on your chair or sofa to complete the look (figs 1 to 3).

❖

No-sew cushion

MATERIALS
sufficient fabric
pinking shears

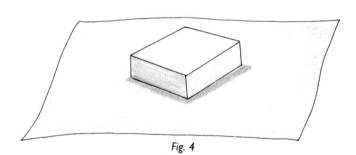

Fig. 4

Method

1 Cut with pinking shears, a rectangle of fabric three times the width of your cushion and twice as wide (fig. 4).

2 Fold the fabric as indicated in the illustration, bringing both ends up to tie in a knot at the top of the cushion (fig. 5). Place the knot to the underside for a tailored look (fig. 6).

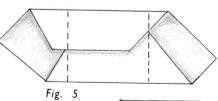

Fig. 5

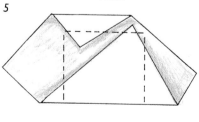

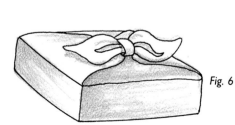

Fig. 6

Table Linen

CIRCULAR TABLECLOTHS

OVERCLOTHS

PLACEMATS AND NAPKINS

QUILTED NAPERY

SCALLOPED NAPERY

FRINGED NAPERY

Table Linen

A grand table set with flowers, china, crystal and silverware can be quite breathtaking. Crisp white linen tablecloths and napkins provide the perfect backdrop against which all the other elements are placed. Linen napkins provide an additional touch of elegance as well as serving a more practical purpose at the dinner table.

All tablecloths and table linen are functional in that they protect your furniture and your clothes from soiling. They can be as decorative as you wish and, depending on the time and place of their use, they can be either casual or formal in style. Their plain, no-fuss construction often means they can also be reversible.

Everyday table linen should be made from easy-care washable fabrics, so that it can survive the stresses of frequent use and the resultant wear and tear. Cotton, polyester and cotton, cotton sateen, gingham and cotton linens are all suitable for casual table linen. Damask and silks add a touch of formality and luxury to a dining table, while a vivid combination of textured fabrics provide a touch of drama.

Contrast and textures create exotic effects even with the most simple of fabrics. Try mixing fabrics, such as linen and satin, to create truly elegant table napkins. Incorporate appliqué or embroidery stitches for an individual look. You can stencil calico napkins with a variety of prints to take you from breakfast to an afternoon tea with a homely country feel.

Instructions for making this elegant table linen are on page 65

The finish you choose will add touches of interest to your table. Layers of mitred corners in a variety of coloured fabrics and textures create a look and style that will leave your guests wondering where you bought the extravagant display.

In a more formal dining room, try to match the table linen to the overall room scheme. For example, use the background colour of your curtains as the base colour for a cloth on a side table to create an interesting harmony of colour and shape in your room. On the other hand, if you want the table to blend into the room, so that a prized vase or collection of china is the focus, select a fabric in a similar colour to your walls, then create an accent with a tandem cloth in a similar texture.

Measuring for tablecloths

❖

When making tablecloths always try to get a fabric that is wide enough to cover the width of the table without seams. You will also need to decide how deep you wish the overhang to be – just to your lap or near to the floor or somewhere in between.

Square tablecloth
Measure across the width of the table. To this measurement, add twice the desired overhang measurement and the hem allowance.

Rectangular tablecloth
Measure across the table. To this measurement, add twice the overhang to find the width of the tablecloth. Measure the length of the table and add twice the overhang to find the length, then add the hem allowance (fig. 1).

Round tablecloth
Measure the diameter of the table through the middle. To this measurement, add twice the desired overhang and the hem allowance.

Oval tablecloth
Measure across the table. To this measurement, add twice the overhang to find the width of the tablecloth. Measure the length of the table and add twice the overhang to find the length. Add hem allowances in each case.

If the width of the table is greater than the fabric width and fabric widths need to be joined, it is important that these joining seams be placed along the table edges and not in the middle.

Joining fabric

❖

You may need to join fabric to achieve the required length and width for a tablecloth. It is important to place these joining seams where they will be as unobtrusive as possible. Usually this means placing them along the table edge (fig. 2). For an oval or a round table place the seams as shown in figs. 3 and 4 below. Always use a flat fell seam when joining fabric so as to avoid thick seams.

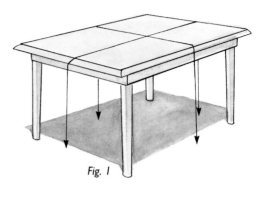

Fig. 1

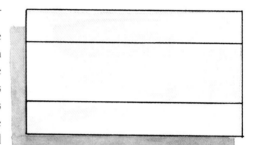

Fig. 2

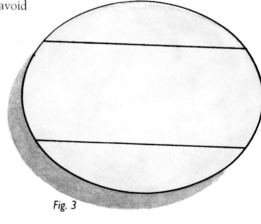

Fig. 3

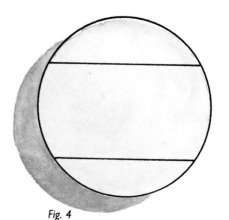

Fig. 4

Circular Tablecloths

CIRCULAR TABLES ARE A PRETTY WAY TO FILL AN EMPTY CORNER. THERE IS NO GREAT MYSTERY TO MAKING CIRCULAR TABLECLOTHS. THE SECRET LIES IN MEASURING AND CUTTING ACCURATELY, THEN THE SEWING IS JUST A STRAIGHT LINE.

Round tablecloth

Before you begin Measure from the centre of the table to the floor. Add extra for a hem if you plan to turn the edge under rather than add a ruffle or lace. Take the edge trimmings into consideration and add or subtract accordingly. This will be your basic measurement. Purchase four times this basic measurement in fabric plus 10 cm. Omit the extra 10 cm if your fabric is as wide as twice the basic measurement or your table is small. Wide sheeting (254 cm wide) is ideal for a tablecloth on a small bedside table because no seams are necessary.

MATERIALS
sufficient fabric
matching sewing machine thread
pins
scissors
tape measure
tailors chalk
sewing machine
trims and ruffles as desired

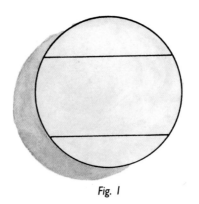

Fig. 1

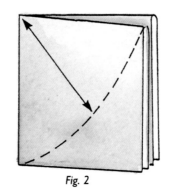

Fig. 2

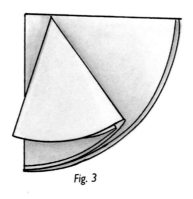

Fig. 3

Method

1 Join your fabric to make one piece large enough for the circle. To do this, cut two pieces, each twice the basic length plus 10 cm. Leave one piece aside. Cut the other piece down through the middle, parallel with both selvages. Using a flat seam, join the selvages of these cut pieces to the selvages of the large uncut piece (fig. 1).

2 To cut out the tablecloth, fold the prepared fabric in half. Fold in half again, so that your original fabric is now folded into quarters. Place one end of the tape measure at the folded point and mark the basic measurement point at one edge of the fabric. Swing the tape measure around, marking out the arc of the circle with the chalk, following the basic measurement point on the tape measure (fig. 2). Cut through all the thicknesses of fabric along this chalk line (fig 3).

3 If you are adding lace, measure around the circumference of the cloth to determine the quantity of ungathered lace or bias binding required. If you are gathering lace or making a fabric ruffle, use at least one and a half times this measurement. For a simple hem, turn in and press 1.5 cm on the edge and stitch. You can stitch narrow piping cord into the hem using the zipper foot on your sewing machine.

Jumbo-edged round cloth

Before you begin Measure your table as for the round tablecloth on page 54. Subtract 4.5 cm from this measurement for the width of the jumbo binding. This is the length of fabric you will require. If necessary, join lengths to achieve the width, using flat fell seams along the edges of the table.

MATERIALS
sufficient fabric

6.5 m of extra-thick piping cord

6.5 m of 10 cm wide bias-cut fabric plus 1.5 cm for each seam allowance

matching or contrasting sewing machine thread

sewing machine

scissors

tape measure

Method

1 Cut out the fabric as for the standard round tablecloth. The raw edges can be overlocked or zigzagged to prevent fraying.

2 Make a continuous bias strip as instructed on page 7. Join the ends of the bias strip to form a circle.

3 Fold the bias-cut fabric over double with the right sides out, enclosing the piping. Using the zipper foot on your sewing machine, sew a row of stitching as close to the piping as possible. Interweave the piping cord ends where they meet (figs. 4 to 6).

4 With the right sides together and the raw edges matching, pin the jumbo piping around the outer edge of the tablecloth, then stitch it in place, following the first stitching line. Trim away any excess seam allowance if necessary. Neaten the raw edge with overlocking or zigzag stitching.

Silk taffeta is the perfect choice for this elegant round cloth

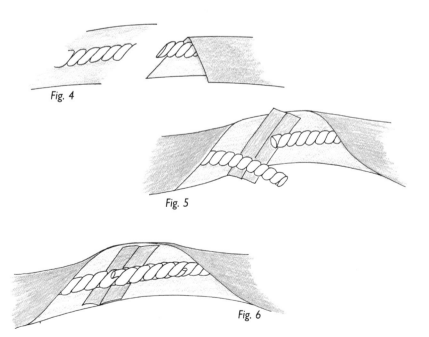

Fig. 4

Fig. 5

Fig. 6

Overcloths

Square overcloth

Before you begin Plan how large you want the overcloth. Make sure the proportion is right for the circular cloth that will be underneath it.

Measuring

To calculate the quantity of fabric you will require, measure the diameter of your table top and add 30 cm for the overhang. For the bias trim, you will need a bias strip of fabric in contrast colour, 4 cm wide and the same length as the sides of the square.

MATERIALS
sufficient fabric
contrasting fabric for bias trim
matching sewing machine thread
scissors
pins
sewing machine
tape measure

Method

1 Make and join the continuous bias strip as shown on page 7. Press in 5 mm on both sides of the bias strip.

2 Cut a perfect square from the fabric to your required measurements. Turn in and press 5 mm, then turn in and press another 5 mm. Stitch the hem in place. Make sure the corners are stitched into neat points.

3 Pin a length of bias strip to two opposite edges of the tablecloth with both the right side of the bias and the right side of the tablecloth facing upwards. Turn in 1 cm on each end of each of the bias strips and secure the ends under the cloth with a pin. Stitch down each side of the bias strip, 2 mm in from each edge. Repeat the process on the other two sides. Press.

For a simple country look, checked cotton can be bias-trimmed following the instructions given here

---

Swagged overcloth

Before you begin You can attach fabric bows to the cloth with Velcro for added effect. Measure the diameter of the table and add to this measurement the overhang and hem allowance you require. You may need to join the fabric as instructed on page 54.

MATERIALS
sufficient fabric
28 cm of 1 cm wide bias binding
40 cm of 75 mm wide elastic
matching sewing machine thread
pins
scissors
tape measure
sewing machine

Method

1 Make the overcloth, following the same method as for making the round tablecloth on page 54. Turn in and press 5 mm around the outer edge, then turn in and press 1 cm. Stitch the hem.

2 Mark the quarter points on the circumference. On the wrong side of the fabric at each of the quarter points and beginning at the edge of the cloth, sew a 7 cm length of bias binding to form a casing. Thread 10 cm of elastic through each casing, stitching the end of the elastic to the outer end of the casing at the cloth edge. Leave the inner end of the casing open. Stitch another length of elastic to the wrong side of the tablecloth, just above the top of the casing. Draw up the elastic in the casing and tie the ends of the two pieces of elastic together, gathering up the casing. Release the elastic for washing and pressing the tablecloth.

festoon overcloth

MATERIALS
circle of fabric

fabric strip for the ruffle, 12 cm wide and twice the circumference of the finished overcloth

fabric, 12 cm x 2 m, for the bows

28 cm of 1 cm wide bias binding

40 cm of 75 mm wide elastic

matching sewing machine thread

pins

scissors

tape measure

sewing machine

Method

1 Make the overcloth, following the method given for the round tablecloth on page 54.

2 Join the ruffle strip with a flat seam to form a circle. Fold the ruffle strip over double with the wrong sides together. Overlock or zigzag the raw edges together. Gather the raw edges together.

3 Pin the ruffle around the bottom edge of the overcloth with right sides together and raw edges even. Adjust the gathering and stitch the ruffle into place.

4 Mark the circumference into quarters. At each of the quarter points stitch a 7 cm length of bias binding to the edge of the wrong side of the overcloth, beginning at the ruffle seams, to form a casing. Thread 10 cm of elastic through each casing, stitching the end of the elastic to the outer end of the casing at the cloth edge. Leave the inner end of the casing open. Stitch another length of elastic to the wrong side of the overcloth, just above the top of the casing. Draw up the elastic in the casing and tie the ends of the two pieces of elastic together, gathering up the casing. Release the elastic for washing and pressing the overcloth.

5 Cut the strip for the bows into quarters. Fold the strips over double with right sides together and raw edges matching. Sew one long side and one short side of each strip. Turn the strips to the right side. Press. Tie the strips into bows and slipstitch into place over the gathering.

Above left: Ruffles and bows make this charming overcloth for a small table

Left: Team the swagged overcloth with chair covers in the same pretty fabric. Make the chair covers in the same way as those on page 47.

Placemats and Napkins

Placemat with contrast border

MATERIALS
*two pieces of main fabric, each
44 cm x 58 cm*

piece of wadding, 44 cm x 58 cm

*approximately 2.10 m of contrasting
fabric for the border*

*1.35 m purchased bias binding
or 3 cm wide bias-cut fabric strip
in a contrasting colour*

matching sewing machine thread

pins

scissors

tape measure

sewing machine

Method

1 Place the main fabric pieces with wrong sides facing and the wadding sandwiched between them. Baste. Quilt through all thicknesses in a pattern of your choice.

2 From the contrasting fabric, cut four strips, two 10 cm x 44 cm and two 10 cm x 58 cm. Turn in and press 1 cm on the long inner edge of each strip. Cut the ends of the strips to perfect diagonals, then join them together with mitred corners (fig. 1).

3 With the right sides facing and the raw edges matching, stitch the border to the main piece. Trim the corners, then turn the placemat through to the right side and press.

4 Press the bias binding over double with the wrong sides together. Tuck the bias binding under the inner pressed edge of the border, leaving 5 mm of the bias binding protruding. Stitch the inner pressed edge down into place, stitching through all thicknesses.

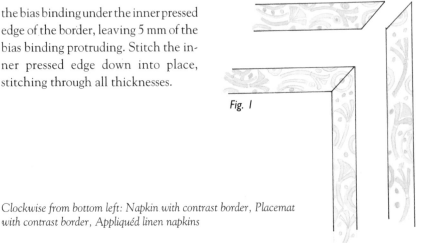

Fig. I

Clockwise from bottom left: Napkin with contrast border, Placemat with contrast border, Appliquéd linen napkins

Appliquéd linen napkins

MATERIALS

piece of fabric, 40 cm x 60 cm, for the basic placemat

60 cm square of fabric, for the basic napkin

fabric motifs for the appliqué

matching sewing machine thread

pins

scissors

tailors chalk

tape measure

sewing machine

Method

1 Cut out the motifs, allowing a 6 mm excess around them.

2 Position the motifs on the placemat and napkin. Baste them in place. Machine-stitch around the edge of each motif, 6 mm from the edge, using a small zigzag stitch. Cut away the excess fabric close to the stitching.

3 Adjust your sewing machine stitch to a wider satin stitch. Stitch again over the previous stitching, enclosing the raw edge as you stitch.

4 Make a narrow double hem around all sides of the napkin. Press.

Satin-stitched napery

Before you begin Measure the size of your table and determine the drop you require, then add 2.5 cm for the hem allowance. Refer to page 53 for further instructions on measuring your table and determining the size of your tablecloth.

MATERIALS

piece of fabric, 32.5 cm x 42.5 cm, for each placemat

32.5 cm square of fabric for each napkin

sufficient fabric for the tablecloth, cut to size

matching or contrasting sewing machine thread

sewing machine

scissors

tape measure

Method

The method is the same for all items.

1 Turn in and press 2.5 cm on all the raw edges, mitring the corners (figs 2 to 4).

2 Machine-stitch a satin stitch border around all sides over the raw edge. Remember to pivot at the corners.

Primary brights in crisp cottons are the perfect choice for these satin stitched napkins and tablecloth

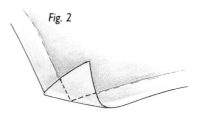

Fig. 2

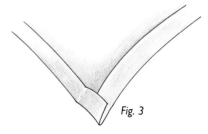

Fig. 3

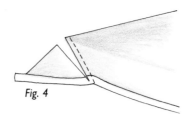

Fig. 4

Napkin with contrast border

MATERIALS
47 cm square of fabric

four strips of contrasting border fabric, each 8 cm x 47 cm (you can vary the width to suit the fabric pattern)

1.8 m of purchased bias binding or 1.8 m of 3 cm wide bias-cut fabric strips

matching sewing machine thread

pins

scissors

tape measure

sewing machine

Method

1 Turn in and press 1 cm along the long inner edge of each border strip. Cut the ends to perfect diagonals, then join them with mitred corners.

2 Place the border strip and the fabric square together so that the right side of the border faces the wrong side of the square. Stitch around the outside edge. Trim the corners, then turn the napkin to the right side and press.

3 Press the bias binding over double with the wrong sides together. Tuck the bias binding under the inner pressed edge of the border, leaving 5 mm of the bias binding protruding. Stitch the inner pressed edge down into place, stitching through all thicknesses.

4 If you are using ribbon or braid which has finished edges, there is a very simple method you can use to achieve the same result. Turn in and press 1 cm on the edges of the napkin, then turn in and press another 1 cm. Stitch. Pin the ribbon or braid around the edge of the napkin, folding the corners as shown (figs 1 to 3). Stitch down close to both edges of the ribbon or braid.

The red and green checked placemat has been made in the same way, omitting the bias binding trim. It has no wadding and is not quilted.

Tartan is terrific for this placemat and napkin

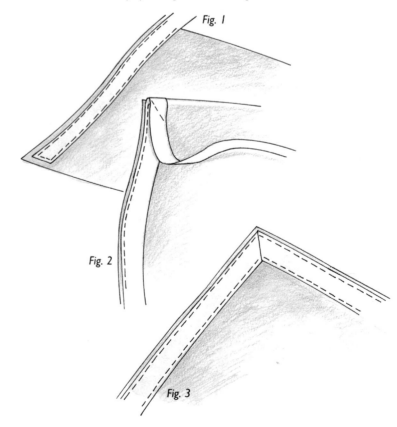

Fig. 1

Fig. 2

Fig. 3

Pleated placemat

MATERIALS

piece of fabric, 30 cm x 137 cm,
for the pleated body

piece of fabric, 10 cm x 160 cm,
for the border strip

fusible interfacing, 30 cm x 90 cm

matching sewing machine thread

sewing machine

pins

thread

tailors chalk or water-soluble marking pen

ruler

Method

1 cm seams are allowed.

1 With the chalk or the pen, mark every 1.5 cm along the length of each long side of the main fabric piece. Begin to fold in the pleats with your fingers and secure the pleats with pins as you go. Pressing with a warm iron will also help to hold the pleats in place while you work. Baste along both edges. The pleated panel should be approximately 25 cm x 40 cm when it is complete.

2 Cut the border into two strips, 10 cm x 30 cm, and two strips, 10 cm x 50 cm. Cut fusible interfacing to the same size and fuse it to the wrong side of the border pieces.

3 Turn in and press 5 mm along the long edges of each border piece. Fold each border piece in half lengthways with wrong sides together and press. Sandwich the pleated centre piece between the folded edges of the border pieces. On the wrong side, overlap the border pieces at the ends so the short and long border pieces meet in an L-shape at the corners (fig. 4). Pin the edges to hold them in place.

4 On the right side, fold the corners to form mitres. Baste through all thicknesses, then machine-stitch in the following way: Begin at the outer edge of one mitred corner, stitch towards the centre down the angle of the mitre then back to the outside edge of the next mitred corner. Repeat the process on the opposite side and then stitch the two remaining inside border edges individually.

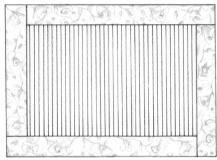

Fig. 4

This unusual pleated effect is very easy to achieve

Quilted Napery

SIMPLE QUILTING IS A FEATURE OF THIS NAPERY.

Before you begin You can quilt your own fabric, using a quilters guide to plan the squares and spaces. The guide looks like an arm that extends from behind the sewing machine's presser foot into the centre of the machine. The first row of stitching is made, then the guide is adjusted to sit along this stitching. Further rows of stitching are made, each the same distance from the previous one, as measured by the guide.

Placemat

MATERIALS
piece of main fabric, 34 cm x 50 cm
piece of wadding, 34 cm x 50 cm
piece of the main fabric or a contrasting one, 34 cm x 50 cm, for the backing
1.8 m of corded piping
matching sewing machine thread
pins
scissors
tape measure
sewing machine

Method

1 Place the main fabric and the wadding together. Pin or baste the layers together and quilt through all thicknesses.
2 Using the rim of a cup as a guide, round off the corners of the main and backing fabric pieces.
3 With the right sides facing and the raw edges matching, pin the piping around the quilted main piece, clipping the seam allowance at the curves for ease. Overlap the ends of the piping where they meet. Draw out a little cord from the piping and cut it off to eliminate bulk. Stitch the piping in place.
4 Place the main and the backing pieces together, with the right sides facing and the raw edges matching. Stitch around the edge, following the previous stitching line and leaving an opening for turning. Turn the placemat to the right side and press. Handsew the opening closed with small stitches.

Napkin

MATERIALS
50 cm square of the main cotton fabric
50 cm square of the contrasting cotton fabric
2.1 m corded piping
matching sewing machine thread
50 cm bias binding in the same colour as the corded piping
pins
scissors
tape measure
sewing machine

Method

1 Using the rim of a cup as a guide, round off the corners of the main and contrast fabric pieces.
2 Make the napkin in the same way as the placemat, omitting the quilting.
3 Fold the bias binding over double, lengthways, with the wrong sides facing and the folded edges matching. Stitch along the folded edges. Knot the ends of the bias binding then stitch the centre 12.5 cm down from one corner of the napkin.
4 Fold the side with the tie attached in half, with wrong sides facing. Roll the opposite side of the napkin towards the end with the tie. Wrap the tie around the rolled napkin and tie it into a bow.

Damper napkin

MATERIALS
piece of fabric, 41 cm x 51 cm
matching sewing machine thread
pins
scissors
tape measure
sewing machine

Method

Overlock or zigzag the fabric edges or turn the hem and then zigzag it in place. Knot the napkin around the damper.

Tea cosy

Before you begin Measure the height and width of your teapot. On a piece of paper, mark the dimensions, allowing an additional 10 cm for seams and turn-under. You will need contrasting bias binding, 6 cm wide by the circumference of the tea cosy plus the length of the arc (see step 1).

MATERIALS
paper
pencil
sufficient quilted fabric
contrasting piping and bias binding
matching sewing machine thread
pins
scissors
tape measure
sewing machine

Method

1 With the dimensions you have calculated, draw your teapot pattern. Draw an arched shape from the centre point to each side point. Cut a front and a back for the tea cosy following this pattern.

2 Pin and baste the piping around the front piece with right sides together and raw edges matching. Pin the front and back together with the right sides facing and the raw edges matching, leaving a 1 cm seam allowance on all the bottom edges. Stitch, catching the piping in the seam.

3 Turn in and press 5 mm on the bottom edges, then turn in and press another 2 cm. Stitch.

4 Bind the bottom edges with the bias binding.

Clockwise from left: Tea cosy, Placemat, Napkin, Damper napkin

Scalloped Napery

THIS SIMPLE BUT ELEGANT TABLECLOTH IS VERY EASY TO ACHIEVE.

MATERIALS

140 cm of 140 cm wide fabric
for the tablecloth

40 cm square of main fabric
for each napkin

matching sewing machine thread

cardboard

marking pen

cup

20 cent piece

water-soluble pen

sharp-pointed scissors

pins

scissors

tape measure

sewing machine

Method

1 To make a template of the scallops on the cardboard, use the twenty cent piece to draw continuous half circles across the edge of the cardboard. Make another template the same way using the edge of the cup. Cut out the templates.

2 For the tablecloth, place the larger template on the edge of the fabric and mark the pattern all along the edge with the water-soluble pen.

3 Using a long close zigzag or satin stitch, work along the scalloped pattern, turning the fabric between each scallop.

4 Using the sharp scissors, cut close to the edge of the stitching, snipping into the scallops as you go. It may also be necessary to run a second row of zigzag stitches over the first, if you want a more dramatic effect.

5 Make the napkins in the same way using the smaller template.

The scalloped edge creates a very elegant appearance

Fringed Napery

UNEVEN WEAVE FABRICS, INCLUDING LINENS AND LOOSELY WOVEN
COTTONS, PROVIDE THE BASE TO CREATE INTERESTING YET VERY SIMPLE
TABLE NAPKINS AND CLOTHS WITH FRINGED EDGES.

This technique works best on a patterned fabric

Before you begin Measure the size of your table. Determine the drop you require for the tablecloth and add 3 cm for the fringing allowance. Fringing works best on a rectangular or square tablecloth.

MATERIALS
*piece of fabric, 32 cm x 42 cm
for each placemat*
27 cm square of fabric for each napkin
*sufficient fabric for the tablecloth,
cut to size*
scissors
pin or needle

Method

1 Ensure that all the fabric edges are as straight as possible.
2 Using a pin or needle, pull out the threads down each long side and then each short side of each piece so that you make approximately 2 cm of fringing on each side. For the tablecloth, make the fringing 3 cm wide.

An Added Touch

Lined Basket

FABRIC LINED BASKETS HAVE MANY USES AROUND THE HOME.

Before you begin If you want the basket to hold books or magazines, ensure that it is wide enough so that books can be laid flat without buckling. If you don't wish to display the contents of your basket, make sure it has high sides or, better still, a lid.

MATERIALS
fabric strip for the side panel, equal to the inside depth of the basket plus 6 cm x twice the inside basket circumference

cardboard and polyester wadding, the same size as the base of the basket

fineline permanent marker pen

piece of fabric, 2.5 cm larger than the inside base of the basket

matching sewing machine thread

ribbon or cord, the same length as the inside circumference of the basket plus 5 cm

fabric strip, 8 cm x 50 cm, for the bow

turning hook or knitting needle

sewing machine, or needle for handsewing

scissors

tape measure

pins

spray adhesive

PVA adhesive

Method

1 Turn the basket over so that the base is facing up. Using the cardboard and marker pen, draw, then cut out a template of the base. Place it inside the basket to check the fit. Remove the template.

2 Using the base template, cut out the wadding. Glue the wadding to the cardboard with a light spray of the adhesive. Using the same template, cut out the fabric for the base, allowing an additional 2.5 cm all around. Lightly spray the wadding with adhesive and fix the fabric to the wadding.

3 When the base cover is dry, turn it over to the reverse side. Snip into the 2.5 cm allowance around the edge of the fabric, then glue the edge of the fabric to the cardboard with the PVA adhesive.

4 Stitch the short ends of the side panel with right sides together to form a circle. Turn in and press 5 mm along the top edge of the side panel, then turn in and press another 4.5 cm. Stitch the hem in place.

5 At the bottom raw edge of the side panel, stitch two rows of gathering stitches 5 mm apart and 1 cm from the edge. Pull up the gathering to fit around the base of the basket. Glue the gathered area of the strip around the base piece, placing the finished edge of the base piece over the gathering.

6 Unpick the seam for 3 cm in the top casing. Thread the length of ribbon or cord through the casing. Place the fabric inside the basket, then using the ribbon or cord, gather in the casing and adjust the gathers evenly around the top edge of the basket. Slipstitch the casing seam closed.

7 Fold the fabric strip for the bow over double with the right sides together and the raw edges matching. Stitch one short edge and one long end. Trim the seams and clip the corners. Turn it through to the right side. Press. Slipstitch the remaining edge closed. Tie the bow around the handle of the basket.

A charming lined sewing basket

Hat Boxes

HAT BOXES PROVIDE EXCELLENT STORAGE FOR A VARIETY OF BITS AND PIECES.

Before you begin How much fabric and wadding you need will depend on the size of your box and whether you are covering it or just lining it. For our fabric-covered box, we used approximately 1.3 m of 115 cm wide fabric and 50 cm of wadding for the lid. Allow an extra 1.5 cm for turn-unders and overlaps around the edges of all the fabric and wadding, unless instructed otherwise.

MATERIALS
sturdy box with a lid
one strip of cardboard, the width of the outer lip of the lid and the same length as the circumference of the outer lip
PVA adhesive
spray adhesive
small paintbrush to apply the adhesive
sufficient fabric
medium thickness polyester wadding
strip of a complementary fabric, 20 cm x 90 cm, for the bow (optional)
braid, ribbon, masking tape or fabric to cover the joins (optional)

Method

1 Cut one lid from the fabric, 2.5 cm larger than the top of the lid all around. Cut one lid from the wadding without any additional allowance. Cut one strip of fabric the circumference of the base by the depth of the box plus 5 cm. Cut one strip of fabric the circumference of the lid by the depth of the lid plus 1 cm. Cut one strip of cardboard the circumference of the lid by the depth. Cut a circle of fabric for the base, 2.5 cm larger all around than the base. Cut one base from the cardboard, without any additional allowance.

2 Glue the wadding on to the lid and centre the fabric piece on top. Clip into the 2.5 cm allowance of the fabric. Glue the clipped allowance down on to the sides of the lid, pulling the fabric quite taut. Trim away any excess fabric.

3 Glue the strip of fabric for the side of the lid to the corresponding strip of cardboard with the 1 cm allowance left free all around. Clip into the allowance, then glue the fabric on one long side and both short ends to the wrong side of the cardboard. Glue the fabric-covered cardboard strip to the outside lip of the lid.

4 Turn in and press one short end of the fabric for the side of the box. Place the fabric around the outside of the box with the turned end covering the raw end and a 2.5 cm allowance at the top and the bottom. Glue into place. Clip into the allowance all around the top and the bottom.

5 Turn the allowance at the bottom of the box over on to the base. Glue into place. At the top of the box, turn the allowance to the inside of the box and glue the allowance into place on the inside.

6 Place the fabric circle for the base face down on a protected surface. Clip into the allowance for 2.5 cm all around the fabric piece. Spray the wrong side of the fabric with adhesive. Place the corresponding cardboard circle on the adhesive and press down. Turn the clipped allowance on to the cardboard and stick it into place.

7 Spray the base of the box with adhesive and glue the fabric-covered cardboard circle on to the base, covering all the raw edges.

8 Cover the joins on the inside of the box with braid, ribbon, masking tape or fabric. Make a bow in the complementary fabric, if desired, and glue it to the lid of the box.

Lampshades

LAMPSHADES ARE AN ESSENTIAL ELEMENT OF MANY DESIGN SCHEMES. AVAILABLE IN AN ARRAY OF SHAPES AND SIZES, THEY WILL BRIGHTEN A DULL CORNER.

Before you begin

The three styles of lampshades shown here are variations on a basic shade, but with individual finishing treatments.

Lampshade frames can be bought from any good craft shop or, if you have existing shades that could do with an update, it's simple to remove the old shade and re-cover the frame yourself. Measure the existing frame to work out quantities of fabric needed.

Always buy a plastic-coated wire lampshade frame to prevent it from rusting over time.

All frames that are to be covered in fabric must be bound with a white or cream cotton tape so that the shade fabric can be stitched to the frame.

Binding the frame

To determine how much binding tape you will need, measure the circumference of the two circles to be covered and all the vertical supporting spokes that connect the two circles. Do not measure the wire or supporting wires where the bulb is to be inserted as these wires will not be covered. Multiply your total length by three to obtain the total length required

To bind the frame: First cover the vertical spokes, tucking the tape under and around the frame (fig. 1). Tuck one end of the tape under the last loop to secure it. Repeat the process for the top and bottom circles so that all the external parts of the frame are covered. In some instances it is easier to secure the tape ends with pins until the binding is complete and then stitch or glue the ends in place.

Stiffened shade

MATERIALS

metal lampshade frame, stripped bare
approximately 1 m of 120 cm wide fabric
approximately 1 m of 120 cm wide buckram iron-on stiffened interfacing
bias strip, 4 cm wide and as long as the combined circumferences of the top and bottom circles plus 2 cm for turnings
PVA adhesive
pegs (optional)
pins
cotton binding tape to cover the frame (see Before you begin)
strong handsewing needle and thread
large piece of paper for the pattern
scissors
fineline marker pen
tape measure

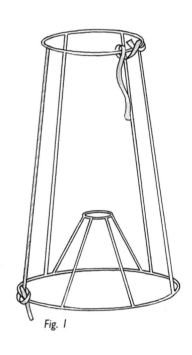

Fig. 1

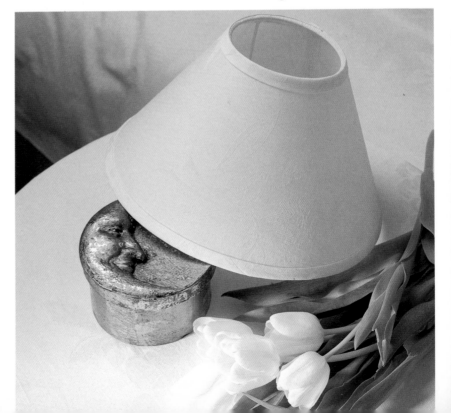

This elegant shade needs no ornamentation

Method

1 Bind the frame as shown.

2 Place the frame at one end of the sheet of paper, then roll the frame across the paper, marking the line with the marker pen to show the outline of the pattern. Cut out the pattern (fig. 2). Check that it fits your frame before cutting out the fabric.

3 Cut out the fabric, allowing 5 mm seam allowances on either end and 5 mm at the top and bottom edges for turnings. Cut the buckram to size.

4 With a warm iron, fuse the buckram to the wrong side of the fabric, leaving all the side turnings free.

5 On both long sides of the bias strip, turn in and press 5 mm.

6 Stitch the bias binding to the top and bottom raw edges of the fabric, with the right sides together, leaving a 1 cm seam allowance on the fabric and stitching in the fold line of the bias binding. If you prefer, you can bind the edges by hand after the fabric has been attached to the frame (fig.3).

7 Press the raw edges of the fabric over the buckram and fit the shade to the frame. Use pegs or pins to keep the shade in place until all the stitching is complete. Fold under 5 mm on one short end and overlap this end over the raw edge where the two ends meet. Glue the overlap. Slipstitch the fabric to the binding on both top and bottom circles.

8 Fold the free side of the bias binding over the frame and slipstitch or glue it into place on the wrong side.

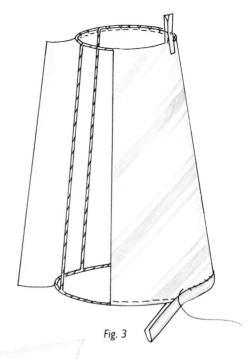

Fig. 3

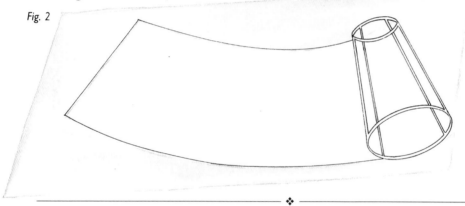

Fig. 2

Pleated shade

Before you begin Measure the circumference of the frame and multiply that measurement by one and a half to give the length of fabric required. Cut bias strips 4 cm wide x the circumference of both circles plus 2 cm for turnings.

MATERIALS
sufficient fabric
metal lampshade frame, stripped bare
approximately 40 cm of fabric for bias strips or purchased bias binding
PVA adhesive
pegs
pins
scissors
cotton binding tape to cover your frame
strong handsewing needle and thread

Method

1 Bind the frame with cotton tape. (See page 70 for more information.)

2 Using your measurements, cut a rectangle of fabric, adding 2 cm to each side for turns. Fold the fabric with the right sides facing and stitch the short ends together in a 2 cm seam. Press the seam open and turn the circle of fabric to the right side.

3 With needle and thread, gather

along the top and bottom edges but do not pull up the gathering.

4 Divide the fabric into four equal sections and mark these points at the top and bottom edges with pins. Place the fabric over the frame, drawing in the gathering threads so that the four pairs of pins are equally spaced around the frame. Use pegs to hold the fabric in position. Arrange the gathered fabric into pleats, evenly spaced around the frame. With your fingers, press the pleats all in one direction and secure them with pins before stitching the pleats into place. Trim any excess fabric.

5 Remove the shade from the frame. Stitch the bias binding to the top and bottom raw edges of the fabric, with the right sides together, leaving a 1 cm seam allowance on the fabric and stitching in the fold line of the bias binding.

6 Place the shade on the frame. Turn the free edge of the bias binding over the frame and slipstitch it in place.

❖

This is a very pretty lampshade for a formal sitting room

We have created this very formal lampshade, following our basic lampshade pattern. Use matching bias binding for the top and bottom trim and a subtly contrasting colour for the centre trim. Apply the two smaller rows of piping so that their seam allowances are touching. Make a third length of 5 cm wide bias binding, turning in and pressing 5 mm on each side. This wider bias strip covers a length of foam cording available from your craft store. Glue the bias to the flat back of the cording and then centre and glue it directly over the top of the bias binding already attached at the base of the shade. Neatly fold under all the ends of the bias to disguise any joins.

Lined shade with ruffle

MATERIALS

metal lampshade frame, stripped bare

approximately 1 m of 115 cm wide fabric
for the cover

approximately 1 m of 115 cm wide
lining fabric

contrasting fabric for bias binding
and ruffles can be cut from scraps,
but if in doubt allow another 40 cm
of fabric for ruffles

large sheet of paper for the pattern

fineline marker pen

PVA adhesive

approximately 6 m narrow cotton tape

handsewing needle and strong
sewing thread

masking tape

scissors

tape measure

Method

1 Bind the frame as instructed on page 70.

2 Place the frame at one end of the sheet of paper, then roll the frame across the paper, marking dots with the marker pen to show the outline of the pattern. Join all the dots and cut out the pattern (see fig. 2 on page 71). Check that it fits your frame before cutting out the fabric.

3 Using the pattern, cut out the lining and main fabric, leaving a 5 cm allowance all around.

4 Fit the lining around the frame, pinning it to the tape. Pin the ends closed as a seam. Remove the lining from the frame and sew the seam as it is pinned. Trim the seam allowance back to 1 cm. Repeat this process for the main fabric.

5 Place the lining inside the frame with the seam following the line of one upright strut. Pin the lining to the binding tape.

6 Cut sufficient 6 cm wide bias strip to go around the top and bottom rings. Turn in and press 1 cm on both long sides of the bias strip, then fold it in half with the wrong sides together. Stitch the binding to the main shade fabric, 1 cm from the edge and stitching in the fold line of the bias binding. Replace shade on the frame. Turn the free edge of the bias binding to the inside and slipstitch it in place.

7 Cut sufficient 10 cm wide ruffle strips which when joined measure at least one and a half or twice the total circumference of the top and bottom rings, depending on the thickness of your fabric. Make each ruffle in the following way: Join the ends of the strip to form a circle. Fold the strip over double with the wrong sides together and the raw edges matching. Overlock or zigzag the raw edges. Gather the raw edges. Draw up the gathering to fit inside the bias-trimmed top and bottom rings. Glue the ruffle into place. Glue the bias binding over the gathered edge, tucking under the short ends at the overlap.

8 Cover the raw edges inside the shade with the masking tape.

A ruffled shade like this needs very little sewing

Towels with flair

A SIMPLE BUT VERY EFFECTIVE DECORATION IN THE BATHROOM IS A STACK
OF PRETTY TRIMMED TOWELS ON AN OPEN SHELF OR DRESSER.

A lace trim turns a plain towel into a very special one

Trimmed towels

Before you begin Across the ends of most towels is a flat, woven band. This is the ideal place to stitch rows of ribbon or braid. You can also stitch lace or scalloped trims under the edge of a length of ribbon or fabric.

Always wash laces before stitching them on so that the trims do not pucker after washing. Remember to trim your face cloths, bath mats and hand towels to match, for a truly coordinated look in your bathroom.

Prewash dark-coloured towels in cold water with cooking salt added to allow for any dye loss. This is especially important if you are working with light-coloured contrasting trims. Prewash the trims to allow for any shrinkage.

To determine how much trim is required for each towel, measure the width of the towel plus 5 cm for turnings.

MATERIALS
towel or item to be covered
trim
matching handsewing thread
needle
pins
scissors

Method

1 If you are using a trim with one finished edge, such as lace, pin the trim on the woven band with the wrong side of the trim facing upwards. Tuck in both raw ends, then stitch along the straight side of the trim, 5 mm from the edge (or at the distance that best suits the design of the trim).

2 Turn the trim to the right side and press. Topstitch along the folded edge, leaving the lacy edge free.

3 If you are using a fabric strip as a trim, turn in and press all the raw edges, then topstitch the trim in place by stitching around all the pressed edges.

Elegant lace-trimmed towels are a feature of this traditional bathroom

---

Appliquéd hand towel

Before you begin For an ensuite bathroom, try this quick and easy appliqué method to coordinate your towels with your bedroom decor, using your bedspread or curtain fabric for the appliqué.

Fusible webbing is a quick and easy method of fusing two layers of fabric together without sewing and is available from fabric and craft shops.

MATERIALS
towel, hand towel, washcloth
fabric with a suitable motif
fusible webbing
scissors

Method

1 Roughly cut out any flower heads or interesting motifs from the fabric.

2 Lay the rough side of the webbing on the wrong side of the motifs. Press for five seconds with a hot dry iron, then let the fabric cool.

3 Carefully cut around the motif. Peel off the backing paper and position the motif on the towel.

Any simple motif can be appliquéd on to a towel

Cover it with a damp cloth and press for a further ten seconds with the iron on the wool/steam setting.

4 It is not essential to machine-stitch, but to make it look like a true appliqué you can outline the motif with a tight zigzag stitch around the outer edge.

Picture Bows

THESE LOVELY ACCESSORIES ARE THE PERFECT FINISHING TOUCH,
BUT DON'T FORGET THEY ARE PURELY DECORATIVE
AND NOT INTENDED TO SUPPORT A WEIGHT.

Bow 1

Before you begin This picture bow has been bagged out in such a way that the lining fabric is visible around the edges of the main fabric.

Determine the length you wish your bow to be, measuring between the point where you would like the bow to sit and 5 cm down behind the picture frame.

Allow an extra 5 cm at the top end for the turned casing that will become the centre of the bow. Determine the width of your bow relative to the frame.

MATERIALS
25 cm of main fabric
30 cm of contrasting fabric
matching sewing machine thread
fabric glue
small hook or ring
sewing machine
pins
scissors
tape measure

Method

1 Cut one main strip to the required width plus 2 cm for seam allowances. Cut the contrasting fabric 2 cm wider.
2 Pin the main fabric and the contrasting fabric together with the right sides facing and the raw edges matching. Stitch the two long sides (fig. 1). Stitch one short side. Trim the seams. Turn the piece through to the right side and press. There should be a narrow border of the contrasting fabric showing on the right side. Slipstitch the open end closed. This is the tail section.
3 To make the centre of the bow, fold the top end of the tail piece over to the front, forming a loop. Topstitch the loop in place; the tighter the loop, the fuller the finished bow will be.
4 Cut a piece of the main fabric, 25 cm x 50 cm, and of the contrasting fabric, 27 cm x 50 cm, for the bow centre. Join the pieces in the same way as for the tail section. At the back of the bow centre, pin and stitch the closed end over the slipstitched end. Slide the bow centre through the loop on the tail section, centring it with the seam under the loop at the back. Secure the bow with a couple of stitches at the back. Sew the hook or ring to the back of the loop.
5 Glue the bottom edge of the tail section to the back of the picture frame. Hang the picture, then attach the bow to a hook on the wall.

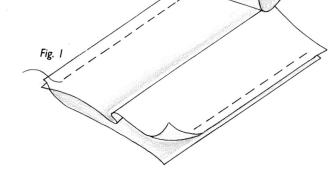

Fig. 1

Method

1 Cut a strip for the bow loop to the required length and width, adding 2 cm for seam allowances. Cut another strip for the bow tails, the same width and the length you have calculated, allowing for the turned casing that wraps around the bow loop.

2 Fold both strips over double with right sides together and raw edges even. Sew the long sides. Turn the strips to the right side through the open ends. Press.

3 Fold the ends of the bow loop so that they meet at the centre back. Slipstitch them together.

4 Fold the tail section in half. Fold 6 to 8 cm at the top over to the front to form the casing. Slipstitch the casing into place. The smaller the casing, the tighter the bow centre will be. Experiment until you are pleased with the effect. Pass the bow loop into the casing so that the slipstitching on the back of the loop falls inside the casing. Slipstitch the loop into place. Sew the ring or hook to the back of the bow.

5 Glue the ends of the tails to the back of the picture. Hang the picture first, then position the bow and attach it to the wall above the picture.

Method

1 Make the tail section in the same way as for bow 1 on page 76.

2 Cut the additional pieces of the main and contrast fabric for the bow centre as for bow 1, but this time cut four pieces instead of two. Make two bow centres as for bow 1.

3 Place the second bow centre over the first and at right angles to it. Stitch them together through the centre. Gather in the bow centres to form a series of tiny gathers in the middle.

4 Gather the square of contrasting fabric and cover the button with it. Stitch the button over the gathers. Secure the bow with a few stitches from the back. Sew the hook or ring to the back of the double bow.

5 Complete as for bow 1.

Bow 2

Before you begin

Determine the length you wish your picture bow to be, measuring between the point where you would like the bow to sit and 5 cm down behind the picture frame. Allow an extra 5 cm at the top end for the turned casing that will become the centre of the bow. Determine the width of your picture bow relative to the width of the frame.

MATERIALS
50 cm of fabric
matching sewing machine thread
small hook or ring
sewing machine
pins
scissors
tape measure

Bow 3

MATERIALS
approximately 25 cm of main fabric
30 cm of contrasting fabric
matching sewing machine thread
fabric glue
small hook or ring
sewing machine
one button to cover
5 cm square of contrasting fabric to cover the button

Drawstring Bag

A DRAWSTRING BAG CAN BE USED FOR MANY DECORATIVE
YET PRACTICAL APPLICATIONS.

Choose a fabric that suits the purpose of your bag

Before you begin Choose a fabric appropriate for the proposed use of the bag; PVC fabric could be used for toiletries, and a light sheer fabric could be used for lingerie. A brightly coloured children's print could be used to take toys to grandma's, or used as a library or book bag, or even for carrying a sleeping sheet to kindergarten. You can make the bag any size you like; the measurements given here are for a toiletry bag.

MATERIALS
60 cm fabric
1.6 m drawstring cord or ribbon
matching sewing machine thread
tailors chalk
sewing machine

Method

1 Fold the fabric over double, lengthways, with the right sides together. Stitch the sides together in a 1.5 cm seam. Neaten the raw edges with overlocking or zigzag stitching.

2 Turn the bag through to the right side. Turn in and press 5 mm at the top edge then turn in and press another 5 cm. Stitch through all thicknesses along the fold and again 1.5 cm away, forming a casing.

3 Open the stitching at the side seams for approximately 1.5 cm. Thread an 80 cm length of cord or ribbon in one opening through the whole casing and out the same opening. Repeat for the other 80 cm of cord or ribbon, threading it through the other opening. Knot the ends of the cord or ribbon together.

Decorative Screen

FABRIC-COVERED SCREENS CAN BE MADE FROM ANY TYPE OF WOOD THAT IS STURDY ENOUGH TO SUPPORT ITS OWN WEIGHT.

Before you begin

If you wish to shape the top of the screen, you will need a jigsaw and a paper pattern to follow when cutting.

MATERIALS
large sheet of paper
pencil
*3 panels of craft wood, each
16 mm x 50 cm x 1.6 m*
jigsaw

5 m of 120 cm wide fabric
1.3 m of 1 to 1.5 cm wide braid
*10 m of 60 cm wide polyester wadding
or 5 mm thick foam*
6 brass hinge brackets and screws
screwdriver
scissors
wood glue
PVA adhesive
spray adhesive
staples and staple gun, or upholstery tacks

Method

1 Make a paper pattern for the curved top of the screen panels. Using the pattern, mark the curve in pencil on top of each panel of craft wood, then cut it out with the jigsaw.

2 Cut two pieces of fabric, each 55 cm x 1.6 m for each panel. Cut two pieces of wadding or foam, each 50 cm x 1.6 m. Using the spray adhesive, glue the wadding or foam to the front and back of each panel.

3 Lightly spray the adhesive on to the wadding, then lay the fabric on top, trimming the top edge in the curved shape of the wood panels with a 2.5 cm allowance.

4 Staple or tack the fabric edges in place. Trim away the excess fabric.

5 Starting at the bottom, turn in the end of the braid, staple or tack it over the fabric edge, then proceed to glue the braid all around each panel, covering the raw edge of the fabric. At the other end, turn under the raw edge of the braid and staple or tack it in place.

6 Attach the hinges. The first hinge should be approximately 20 cm from the bottom and the other hinge should be approximately 20 cm from the top of the screen.

Use a screen to divide a room, provide a private space or hide what you don't want to be seen

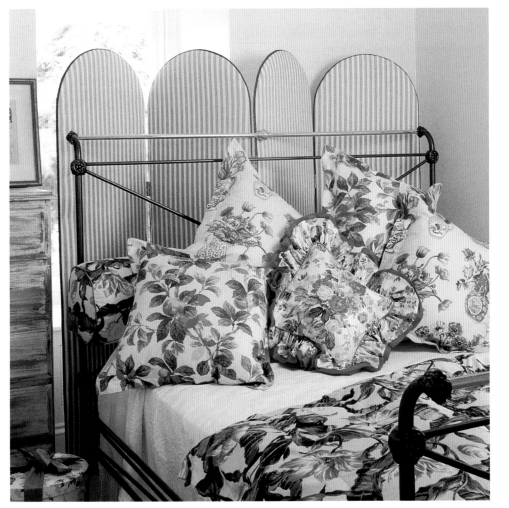

Index